Wild Game Cookbook

by John A. Smith

DOVER PUBLICATIONS, INC., NEW YORK

"It takes more than the eating of one brook trout
To make one an epicure out and out."

(Cratinus. Flourished from about 480-423 B.C.)

Published in Canada by General Publishing Company, Ltd., 30 Lesmill Road, Don Mills, Toronto, Ontario.
Published in the United Kingdom by Constable and Company, Ltd.

Wild Game Cookbook is a new work, first published by Dover Publications, Inc., in 1986. Some of the recipes in the present volume were previously published in various publications by Hollybrooke Press, Foster City and Belmont, California.

Manufactured in the United States of America
Dover Publications, Inc., 31 East 2nd Street, Mineola, N.Y. 11501

Library of Congress Cataloging in Publication Data

Smith, John A.
    Wild game cookbook.

    1. Cookery (Game) I. Title.
TX751.S64   1986   641.6'91   86-2188
ISBN   0-486-25127-6

To Brooke and Holly

our critics
our judges
our pleasures
our happiness

our daughters

The Game Master

You have had a great day in the field. Your bag is filled with game and you are relaxing by your campfire. Steaming cup of coffee in hand, you watch the sun dwindle in a fire-red sea on the western horizon as long, purple shadows soften the rose-tipped hills and snow-crested mountains. Your dog lays his head on outstretched paws and sighs a deep and mighty sigh as he stares into the glowing fire.

It is that magic hour at the end of the hunt.

Soon you will have to do something with all that beautiful game. But what?

Some of us hunters are fortunate enough to be married to that special kind of woman who understands and enjoys both hunting and cooking wild game. Some of us are able to create mouth-watering dishes at home and in the field with our bounty from field and stream. All too many, however, do not know what to do with the game. Some of it gets cooked, some gets given away, and some even gets thrown (foolishly) away.

It is the purpose of the WILD GAME COOKBOOK to show you how to become a wild game cook par excellence, and how to prevent waste of wild game. This collection of recipes was gathered and tested during more than thirty years of hunting and fishing all over the world. Some of these recipes have been handed down through several generations of my family. Many have been designed for use in the hunt camp where the beautiful Dutch oven is the basic, and often only, implement used.

Good hunting! Better eating!!

J.A.S.

Contents

Contents

v

Contents

Introduction

When was the last time you heard someone say:

"Venison is too gamey for me."

"Wild duck tastes too fishy."

"Pheasant is so dry."

"Wild goose tastes like it was cooked in mud."

"Quail (rabbit, dove, etc.) is just plain tough.'

"Antelope is only good for stew meat."

Maybe they were right!

If they were right, the hunter and the cook pooled their lack of knowledge to place that sort of food on the table.

The hunter didn't learn or know how to field-dress his kill. To make matters worse, he may even have tied the carcass of his "trophy" deer across the hood of the car, exposing it to the elements and the noxious exhaust of cars and trucks, as he drove a few hundred miles homeward.

The cook didn't learn or know how to butcher and prepare the game, compounding this error by

Introduction

ignoring the subtleties of seasoning, the delicacy of wild game flavor, and the careful control of temperature.

It is NOT the purpose of this book to teach you how to dress your game, (there are many good books on this subject available in bookstores and at the U.S. Department of Fish and Game), but it IS the purpose of this book to teach you the preparation and cooking skills so very important to the cook.

Most of the recipes included in this book are for camp or home cooking using oven, skillet, or Dutch oven. We have also included several electric slow cooker recipes, having learned that this cooker is ideal for those recipes requiring long, slow cooking.

Many standard recipes can be converted to electric slow cooker recipes, especially those created for the Dutch oven. You will find that seasoning takes on a new dimension through this cooking process. Care must be taken to prevent strong herbs and seasonings from overpowering the other ingredients. Liquid measures, because there is very little or no evaporation, must be greatly reduced in this type of cooking.

A note of caution: For convenience, we have listed the number of servings each recipe yields. They should be taken as an approximate indication only, as servings can vary considerably according to the size of the game, the appetite of the company and the number of dishes offered with the entrée. Similarly, cooking time can vary depending on the age and condition of the animal involved. So be on your toes, and use your own best judgment.

Preparing Game

The quality of furred and feathered game is directly related to the age of the animal and the diet of its environment. This is best demonstrated by the flavor of duck raised in a coastal delta environment which imparts a somewhat fishy taste to the bird. Cattle, for example, may be range fed or grain fed. Deer may sometimes subsist on tender pine shoots, sometimes on native grass, and sometimes on pungent forest herbs. These variations in diet have much to do with the flavor of the game.

When preparing wild deer, the carcass must always be bled, cooled, and field-dressed as soon as possible. The cavity should be protected from insect invasion and the cooled carcass wrapped with cheese cloth or other material to protect it during the trip from field to kitchen.

Much large game is ruined during the field-dressing stage before it ever reaches the kitchen. The internal organs and intestines contain strong acids which, if permitted to spill on the flesh, ruin it for any use. The hunter must take care to insure these organs are not pierced and that the animal's hair is kept free of exposed flesh at all times.

Aging the meat will impart tenderness. Venison, for example, should be hung for about two weeks at temperatures just above freezing before it is butchered. It can then be cut, packaged, and frozen for future use. However, almost all game meat should be consumed within the first six to nine months of freezing in order to enjoy its texture and flavor.

The most tender cuts of venison come from the area of the back and saddle. Shoulder and leg cuts should be used for low temperature, moist, long cooking time recipes only. The animal fat found in wild game is almost always excessively pungent and should be carefully removed before cooking. The game is, therefore, usually larded before cooking, or oils are added to the recipe

Preparing Game

during cooking to substitute for the missing fat.

One of the best ways to remove the gamey taste of venison is to soak the meat in a mixture of salt, vinegar and water overnight. Use ¼ pint of vinegar to 1 gallon of water, stirring in 4 tablespoons of kosher salt.

Wild duck raised in delta areas feed on a variety of fish and sea animals. To remove this fishy flavor, simply soak the cleaned and plucked carcass in milk overnight. Stuff the carcass cavity with a mixture of onion and lemon, refrigerating overnight (see Flavor Insurance in the section on Wild Duck). Never use metal bowls or pots when soaking or marinating game.

Some game animals have musk glands which exude a powerful acid that quickly ruins the game if not carefully removed. The gall bladder in birds must also be carefully removed in order to avoid rupture and definite spoilage of the meat.

If you plan to do a great deal of wild game cooking, it is advisable to have available a large store of blanched salt pork or bacon fat. This is used for barding during cooking. Cut into thin sheets or slices, it is laid over a bird's breast or inserted into the meat with a larding needle or dull-pointed instrument. This barding is removed prior to the completion of cooking to permit the meat to become delicately browned.

Stocks and Soups

Stocks and Soups

If you are truly "into" wild game and wish to present the finest quality of game fare to your guests, you have probably already learned that it is wasteful and foolish to throw away scraps left over from butchering your game, or scraps left in the serving dish. These should be saved and used in stocks, soups and garnishes. Nothing seems to be as warming, rewarding and filling as a bowl of steaming soup taken in a cold duck blind. And an accomplished game cook wouldn't think of cooking game and making sauces without a good game stock supply, which can also be converted to a richly aromatic soup. The game cook can quickly combine stock with various vegetables and selected seasonings in a blender to create an excellent soup. A liaison of beaten egg yolks and cream may be added to thicken and enrich the soup if the stock used is too thin.

When making the game stock, little or no salt is added to the basic recipe, as it is usually added to the recipes in which the stock is later used. If the stock contains a high quantity of garlic, onions or strong herbs, it should not be frozen and kept longer than a month or it will develop a strong flavor overpowering the recipe in which it is used.

If the stock is to be frozen and saved for later use, it should be reduced by simmering with the cover off the pot until a concentrate of broth remains. This concentrate can then be frozen into ice cubes or 1-cup size plastic bags for use either in the kitchen or in the field. The addition of water will return the stock to its desired strength.

Many recipes in the WILD GAME COOKBOOK call for game stock, and many delicious and inexpensive soups can be made from it.

BASIC GAME STOCK   Makes 1 gallon
(Venison or Beef)

2	pounds lean meat, cubed
2	pounds bones
2	carrots, sliced
2	large onions, sliced
2	stalks celery, sliced
1	clove garlic
1	cup dry white wine

4	quarts water
½	tsp dried thyme
1	bay leaf
3	sprigs parsley
2	Tbsp tomato paste
1	tsp MSG (optional)
	salt

★ Preheat the oven to 450°F.

★ Put the meat, bones, and vegetables in a large roasting pan. Roast in preheated oven for 15 minutes, uncovered.

★ Transfer the contents of the roasting pan to a deep kettle. Add the remaining ingredients. Bring to a boil and quickly reduce heat to simmer. Slowly simmer for four hours without additional seasoning. Periodically remove all surface scum.

★ Strain the reduced stock through damp cheesecloth. Taste for seasoning, but remember that you will add salt in most subsequent recipes.

Stocks and Soups

JACK'S GAME STOCK   Makes about 2 quarts

This recipe can be prepared with game at hand or with chicken.

2	pounds of backs, necks, and giblets	½	tsp dried thyme
1	pound of cracked bones	1	bay leaf
2	carrots, sliced	3	sprigs parsley
2	large onions, sliced	1	tsp MSG (optional)
2	celery stalks, sliced	1	sprig fresh sage
		4	juniper berries
1	garlic clove	1	cup dry white wine
3	peppercorns	3	quarts cold water
		2	Tbsp tomato paste

★ Preheat oven to 450°F.

★ In a large roasting pan, roast together the meat, bones, and vegetables in preheated oven for 15 minutes.

★ Transfer to a deep kettle. Add the remaining ingredients. Over medium heat, bring slowly to a boil. Simmer over low heat for 4 hours, continually removing any scum.

★ Strain the broth through a damp cheesecloth.

★ Remember that this stock will be used for making sauces in which it will usually be reduced, so seasoning is not critical at this point. Salt and pepper can be added in later use.

★ To thicken the stock, bring 2 quarts of strained stock to a boil. Combine 3 Tbsp cornstarch with 3 Tbsp water and stir them into the boiling stock. Blend well and let simmer for a few minutes.

GAME STOCK SOUP   **Serves 4**
(For clear game stocks)

3	eggs, slightly beaten
2	Tbsp cold water
2	Tbsp finely chopped parsley
¼	cup freshly grated Parmesan cheese
¼	tsp nutmeg
4	cups clear, well seasoned game stock

★ Mix the eggs, cold water, parsley, Parmesan cheese and nutmeg together.

★ In a large pot, bring the game stock to a boil. Pour in the egg mixture in a steady stream while stirring with a large fork

★ As soon as the egg mixture has set, taste for seasoning and serve.

Stocks and Soups

DUCK SOUP   Serves 2 as a meal, 4 as a soup course

Duck soup may be made with stock from any wild game, but duck stock is preferred.

5	cups game stock		4	Tbsp dry sherry
	herb sack (1 bay leaf, 3 sprigs parsley,		½	cup diced duck meat
	1 sprig thyme)		¼	tsp lemon juice
1	onion, diced			
2	small carrots, diced			chopped parsley
2	stalks celery, sliced			
1	tsp MSG (optional)			
1	Tbsp red currant jelly			

★ Skim the fat from the game stock.

★ Strain the stock into a large pot. Add the herbs, vegetables and MSG. Cook and simmer for 40 minutes or until vegetables are tender. Do not let the stock boil or it will become cloudy.

★ Add the red currant jelly and let dissolve.

★ Remove the herb sack. Add the sherry and diced duck meat. Heat thoroughly.

★ Season to taste and add the lemon juice.

★ Sprinkle with chopped parsley and serve hot.

PHEASANT SOUP   Serves 4

This soup recipe was discovered during a hunting trip to Sterling, Colorado, where the soup was made in a Dutch oven over an open fire. There was snow on the ground, but four hunters were warmed thoroughly with this delicious hunting-camp soup.

1 pheasant carcass	1 small bay leaf
6 cups water	4 peppercorns
1 onion, sliced	
2 carrots, sliced	4 mushrooms, diced
2 stalks celery, sliced	1 Tbsp minced chives
salt and pepper	
½ tsp MSG (optional)	½ cup diced, cooked pheasant meat
3 sprigs parsley	½ cup dry sherry

★ Break the carcass into several pieces. Place in the pot with the water, onion, carrots and celery. Season with salt and pepper and stir in the MSG. Add the parsley, bay leaf and peppercorns.

★ Cover and cook slowly for 45 minutes.

★ Strain the stock through cheese cloth or a fine sieve.

★ Add the mushrooms and chives to the stock and cook for 5 minutes. Add the pheasant meat and heat thoroughly. Add the sherry.

★ Taste for seasoning and serve hot.

Dove and Pigeon

The western grain fields teem with dove during the fall, and millions of dollars are spent on guns, ammunition, fuel and equipment used in the hunt for Whitewing and Mourning Dove. The game is plentiful and the taste delightful, if the hunter and cook use care in field–dressing and preparing the birds for the table.

While some hunters will go through the exercise of plucking the birds, there is little useable meat other than the breast. We clean the birds in the field, stripping out the breast and cleaning it off with dry grass before dropping it into a plastic game sack. Watch out for the gall bladder! Rupture it and you will spoil the meat.

Pigeons, being larger than dove, can be plucked and stuffed, but are rarely prepared this way in America. Even in England, where wild wood pigeon are plentiful, they are usually skinned and quartered.

If dove or pigeon are frozen, they should be consumed within a maximum period of six months. Frozen birds may be thawed overnight in the refrigerator or placed in a large bowl and covered with milk. This milk bath restores the texture of the flesh and removes any undesirable flavors.

CAJUN DOVE   **Serves 3 to 4**
A Dutch Oven Recipe for Camp Cooking

15	dove	3	large white onions, chopped
	lard	2	cloves garlic, minced
1	cup all-purpose flour	½	cup bell pepper, minced
1	tsp salt		boiling water
1	tsp freshly ground black pepper	1	cup rosé wine

★ Place the Dutch oven on a grate over the fire, preferably hot coals.

★ Add enough lard to provide about 1" in the bottom of the pot.

★ In a paper bag, combine the flour, salt and pepper. Shake the birds in the bag until well coated.

★ Brown the birds in the hot lard. Remove from the pot and pour off all but about 2 Tbsp hot lard.

★ Add the onions and sauté until very soft, stirring constantly.

★ Add the garlic and bell pepper. Sauté until soft.

★ Return the birds to the pot. Add the wine and enough boiling water to cover the birds. Taste for seasoning and cover the pot.

★ Move the Dutch oven to a place on the grill where it will simmer slowly. Cook, covered, for 2 hours.

★ Remove the birds. Thicken the pan juices with flour, heat and serve over the birds on a bed of brown rice.

Dove and Pigeon

DAD'S DOVES   A Campsite Recipe for 2 Hunters

6 to 8 dove
⅓ cup flour
½ tsp salt
¼ tsp black pepper

½ cup olive oil
1 clove garlic, crushed

1 cup Beaujolais wine
water

2 Tbsp dry white wine
1 Tbsp all-purpose flour

★ Dust the birds with flour seasoned with salt and pepper.

★ In a heavy skillet, heat the oil and lightly sauté the crushed garlic.

★ Add the birds and lightly brown. Remove the garlic and discard.

★ Add the red wine and just enough water to barely cover the birds. Simmer for 1½ hours or until tender.

★ Remove the birds to a heated platter. Mix the white wine with the 1 Tbsp flour and stir into the pan juices to thicken. Taste for seasoning and return the birds to the sauce. Serve over wild rice.

Dove and Pigeon

MESS O' BIRDS   **Serves 2 to 4**
A Dutch Oven Camp Recipe

8 to 10 birds—dove, quail, etc.

4   **slices bacon**

1   **onion, chopped**

½   **cup all-purpose flour**
½   **tsp salt**

½   tsp black pepper

1   **large can sauerkraut, drained**
1   **tsp caraway seeds**
1   **small can pitted black olives**

1   **cup dry white wine (or 1
      can beer)**

★ Place the Dutch oven over the campfire. Fry the bacon and remove. Drain and crumble, reserving for future use.

★ Sauté the onion in the hot bacon grease.

★ Combine the flour, salt and pepper in a paper bag. Shake the birds in the flour mixture.

★ Brown the birds in the hot bacon grease and onion. Toss the sauerkraut, caraway seed and olives together. Pour over the birds.

★ Pour the cup of wine over the contents. Cover and cook for 30 minutes.

★ Add the bacon bits, stir in, cover and cook for an additional 10 minutes.

★ Serve hot with thick slices of sourdough bread.

Dove and Pigeon

DELICIOUS DOVE   Serves 2
For Dutch Oven

12 dove breasts
½ cup all-purpose flour
  salt
  freshly ground black pepper

1 stick butter

1 cup mushroom caps
1 cup celery, finely chopped

1 cup carrots, diced
½ cup onion, minced

1 cup boiling water
½ cup rosé wine
1 8 oz. can mushroom sauce

★ Mix the flour, salt and pepper in a paper bag. Dredge the breasts.

★ Melt the butter in a Dutch oven. Brown the breasts on all sides. Remove and reserve the birds.

★ Sauté the mushroom caps in the remaining butter. Remove and reserve. Sauté the vegetables.

★ Return the mushrooms to the sautéed vegetables. Add the boiling water and wine. Stir in the mushroom sauce.

★ Add the dove breasts. Cover and bake in a preheated 350°F oven for 1 hour.

DUTCH OVEN DOVE   **Per serving**

6 dove breasts	1 onion, finely chopped
½ cup all-purpose flour	1 cup sliced mushrooms
½ tsp salt	1 Tbsp parsley
½ tsp pepper	½ cup dry white wine
2 Tbsp butter	½ cup heavy cream

★ Wash and dry the breasts. Mix the flour, salt and pepper together in a paper bag. Dust the breasts well by shaking them in the flour bag.

★ Heat the butter in a Dutch oven. Sauté the breasts lightly in the butter. Remove and keep warm.

★ Sauté the onion, mushrooms and parsley in the butter remaining in the Dutch oven. Return the breasts, pouring the wine over them. Cover and cook for 30 minutes, stirring occasionally.

★ Add the heavy cream. Stir and let heat for 10 minutes. Serve hot.

Dove and Pigeon

DOVE APRICOT   **Serves 2**
For Camp or Home

6 to 8 dove	½ cup game stock or chicken broth
flour	½ cup apricot nectar
salt	2 tsp cornstarch
pepper	1 Tbsp honey
¼ cup butter	

★ Dust the birds with flour seasoned with salt and pepper.

★ In a heavy skillet, heat the butter and lightly brown the birds. Cover and simmer for 40 minutes. Remove to a heated platter.

★ Combine the game stock, apricot nectar and cornstarch. Add to pan drippings. Stir in the honey. Simmer until the sauce thickens slightly and bubbles.

★ Pour the sauce over the birds and serve.

GOPHER GUS' DELIGHT   Serves 2

4 to 6 small game birds

1 cup all-purpose flour
½ tsp salt
½ tsp freshly ground black pepper

1 stick butter

½ cup finely chopped onion
½ cup cross-cut celery
1 Tbsp parsley
½ cup Rhine wine
1 Tbsp honey

½ cup heavy cream

★ Split the birds down the back. Wash and dry.

★ In a paper bag, mix the flour, salt and pepper. Drop the birds into the bag and shake until well coated.

★ Over medium heat, melt the butter in a Dutch oven or casserole. Lightly brown the birds and remove to a heated platter.

★ Sauté the onion, celery and parsley in the remaining butter in the Dutch oven. Mix the wine and honey, adding to the sautéed vegetables.

★ Return the birds to the vegetable mixture. Stir in, cover and cook at 325°F for 1 hour and 30 minutes.

★ Uncover and stir in the heavy cream off the heat. Do not boil. Cover and cook for an additional 15 minutes. Serve hot.

Dove and Pigeon

PIGEON STEW   Serves 4

This recipe was adapted from one found in the cookbook *Housekeeping In Old Virginia*, published in 1879, and is still one of the best recipes for pigeon. The unknown cook explained it in these words:

"The pigeons must be seasoned with pepper, salt, cloves, mace and sweet herbs. Wrap the seasoning in a piece of butter and put it in the pigeon. Then tie up the neck and vest and half roast the pigeons. Then put them in a stewpan with a quart of good gravy, a little white wine, some pickled mushrooms, a few peppercorns, three or four blades of mace, a bit of lemon peel, a bit of onion and a bunch of sweet herbs. Stew until done, then thicken with butter and yolks of eggs. Garnish with lemon."

We explain it in these words:

4 pigeons	½ cup dry white wine
¾ tsp salt	1 medium onion, chopped
¾ tsp pepper	1 herb sack (½ bay leaf, ½ tsp thyme,
½ tsp ground clove	1 sprig parsley)
½ tsp mace	½ lemon peel, finely diced
½ tsp marjoram	
thyme	1 cup pickled or canned mushrooms
4 pats butter	
	2 egg yolks
4 cups chicken gravy	1 Tbsp butter ▶

22

Dove and Pigeon

★ Combine salt, pepper, clove, mace, marjoram and pinch of thyme. Mix ¼ of this with each pat of butter.

★ Place the butter balls in the cavities and sew up the birds.

★ Place the birds in an earthware casserole or Dutch Oven. Roast in a pre-heated 325°F oven for 20 minutes, uncovered.

★ Add the gravy, wine, onion and herb sack. Sprinkle with lemon rind. Cover and cook for 2 hours, stirring at the end of each ½ hour period.

★ Add the mushrooms. Cover and cook for an additional 30 minutes.

★ Transfer the pigeons to a heated platter. Remove and discard the herb sack.

★ Mix the egg yolks with 1 Tbsp melted butter. Stir into the liquids in the pot to thicken. Pour over the pigeons and serve.

PAISANO PIGEON   **Serves 4**

4   wild pigeon
⅔   cup all-purpose flour
2   tsp salt
    freshly ground black pepper
¼   cup safflower oil
1   pound can tomatoes

2   onions, sliced
1   bell pepper, sliced
½   cup sliced mushrooms
1   clove garlic, minced
1   bay leaf
4   sprigs parsley ▶

Dove and Pigeon

★ Split and quarter the pigeons. Mix the flour and salt. Coat the pigeon pieces and lightly sprinkle with freshly ground pepper.

★ Heat the safflower oil in a large skillet. Brown the birds evenly on all sides.

★ Add the tomatoes, onion, bell pepper, mushrooms, garlic, bay leaf and parsley. Cover and cook over low heat for 30 minutes, or until tender.

★ Uncover and cook for 15 minutes. Remove the parsley and bay leaf. Serve.

SHERRY SQUAB   Serves 4

4 squab, halved lengthwise	salt
2 Tbsp butter	freshly ground black pepper
1 Tbsp minced onion	$\frac{1}{3}$ cup dry sherry
$1\frac{1}{2}$ tsp chicken-flavor gravy base	2 tsp cornstarch
$\frac{1}{2}$ cup hot water	

★ Heat the butter in a large skillet. Lightly brown the squab halves for 10 minutes.

★ Add the onion, gravy base and hot water. Lightly season with salt and pepper.

★ Cover and simmer for 30 minutes. Remove the squab to a heated platter. Skim the excess fat from the pan juices.

★ Combine the sherry and cornstarch, blending well into the pan juices. Cook and stir until thick and bubbling. Pour the sauce over the birds and serve.

SWEET 'N SOUR PIGEON   Serves 4

4   wild pigeon, quartered
¼ cup butter

¼ cup garden green onions, sliced
¼ cup pineapple chunks

2   Tbsp pineapple syrup
¼ cup tarragon vinegar
¼ tsp salt

★ Melt the butter in a large skillet. Brown the squab evenly on all sides.

★ Add the onion and pineapple chunks. Cook until the onion is tender but not browned.

★ Combine the pineapple syrup, vinegar and salt. Add to the skillet and stir in. Cover and simmer 30 minutes or until tender. Serve from the skillet.

Wild Duck

Wild Duck

Wild duck is perhaps the most maligned game we have encountered. People along the coastal waterways tell us the bird tastes "fishy" and some along the central rivers and streams complain of a "muddy taste." We understand these problems, but find that, be it Teal or Mallard, Butterball or Spoonbill, wild duck can be every bit as delicious and tender as domestic duck.

Some of my duck hunting friends prefer their birds roasted quickly with high heat, the flesh being very rare and juicy. Others prefer to fillet the breast meat and sauté or fry in butter and seasonings.

We prefer to roast the entire bird at moderate temperatures, permitting time to infuse the meat with flavor and the stuffing with moisture as well as flavor. If your duck is an adult or old bird, simply roast until tender - but don't overcook! While the duck is roasting, cook wild rice in lightly seasoned game stock or consommé and you will have the basic meal most honored among duck hunters. You need only a tart jelly, a green vegetable and salad of your choice.

The opening statement of this section addresses the problem of duck tasting "fishy" or "muddy." Domesticators of the bird learned early that diet had a lot to do with both its flavor and tenderness, and that the wild bird's diet caused an unpalatable muddy or fishy taste. This taste is, however, easily removed if you follow these simple instructions:

Flavor Insurance

Pluck and clean the duck. Rub the cavity lightly with a cloth dampened in vinegar. For each duck, slice one onion and mix with ¼ chopped lemon. Stuff the cavity with the onion and lemon mixture. Refrigerate overnight. When ready to cook, discard the stuffing . . . its job is done.

28

BASIC DUCK   Serves 2

    2   ducks
    1   large can sauerkraut (about 28 ounces)
    2   cups Burgundy wine
    1   cup orange juice

★ Marinate the sauerkraut in the wine for ½ day. Drain the sauerkraut and mix with the orange juice (fresh is preferred). Stuff the cavities with the sauerkraut/orange juice mixture.

★ Sew up the birds. Cut off the wing tips and truss.

★ Place the birds on a trivet in an uncovered baking pan or Dutch oven. At low temperature (325°F oven) roast slowly until tender.

DARLIN' DUCK   Serves 2

    2   ducks (Canvasbacks)
        vinegar
    ⅓   stick butter per duck

        freshly ground black pepper
        salt
    1   tsp thyme
    2   Tbsp Worcestershire sauce
    1   tsp sweet basil

    1   tsp oregano
    1   large pinch red pepper
    1   whole onion, chopped
    1   cup chopped celery
    1   cup chopped green pepper
    ½   cup dry white Rhine wine
    2   cups game stock

    2   oranges ▶

29

Wild Duck

★ Lightly scrub the ducks with a cloth dipped in vinegar. Place the butter in the cavities. Lay the birds, breast up, in a baking dish.

★ Sprinkle generously with freshly ground black pepper and salt. Mix together all ingredients, except the oranges and pour over the ducks.

★ Preheat the oven to 350°F. Cook for 2 hours, basting frequently with the liquids in the baking dish.

★ Squeeze the oranges, reserving the rinds. Chop the rinds and add to the orange juice.

★ Add the orange juice and rinds to the liquid in the baking dish. Pour the mixture over the ducks. Cook for an additional 90 minutes. Increase oven temperature to 400°F, cooking for another 20 minutes.

BAYOU GUMBO   Serves 2

2 ducks (3 teal)	pepper
½ cup safflower oil	Louisiana hot sauce
	2 Tbsp Worcestershire sauce
all-purpose flour	1 turnip, peeled
2 onions, chopped	1 bay leaf
1 bell pepper, chopped	
2 cloves garlic, minced	2 pounds smoked sausage
1 cup hot water	½ pint oysters
	3 shallots, chopped
1 tsp salt	1 Tbsp minced parsley
	filé gumbo

▶

Wild Duck

★ Heat the oil in a Dutch oven. Cut the duck into eating pieces and brown in the oil.

★ Remove the duck and add flour to make a roux. Stir until very dark, but do not burn. Quickly add the onions, bell pepper and garlic. Stirring, cook the mixture down until the vegetables are very soft.

★ Add the cup of hot water and stir in. Add the browned duck and stir in enough additional hot water to cover all the duck pieces.

★ Bring to a slow boil. Season with salt, pepper, Louisiana hot sauce and Worcestershire sauce. Add the turnip and bay leaf. Cover and cook for 1 hour.

★ Brown the sausage, drain, cut into bite size pieces and add to the gumbo.

★ Cook, covered, for 20 minutes. Add the oysters, shallots and parsley. Cover and cook for about 15 minutes longer, or until the oysters are shriveled. Serve over brown rice and sprinkle with filé gumbo.

Wild Duck

DAD'S DUCK Serves 1 to 2

1 duck

2 cups applesauce (1 can)
1 tsp grated nutmeg
1 tsp ground cinnamon
1 Tbsp sugar

salt
freshly ground black pepper

3 Tbsp vinegar

3 Tbsp butter
1 tsp honey
4 peppercorns, crushed

½ cup apple jelly

2 pippin apples
flour
1 stick butter
1 Tbsp white rum

★ Preheat oven to 375°F.

★ Sprinkle the applesauce with the nutmeg, cinnamon and a little sugar. Mix well. Let sit until most of the liquid has evaporated.

★ Stuff the duck with the applesauce mixture. Sew the cavity tightly closed.

★ Rub the bird with salt and pepper.

★ Combine the vinegar, butter, honey and crushed peppercorns in a saucepan. Bring to a boil. Baste the duck with this mixture frequently while roasting.

★ Roast the bird 15 minutes per pound.

★ Remove the duck to a heated platter. Stir the apple jelly into the pan juices. Brush the duck with the sauce. ▶

32

★ Cut the apples in half. Peel and core them. Dust with flour.

★ Heat the stick of butter in a frying pan and sauté the apples until golden. Add 1 Tbsp rum while sautéeing. Serve with the duck.

DANDY DUCK   **Serves 2**

For the Dutch Oven

1 Mallard	1 Tbsp cornstarch
¼ cup safflower oil	1 Tbsp grated orange rind
2 slices bacon	1 cup orange juice
	¼ tsp salt
1 cup Burgundy wine	pepper
⅓ cup brown sugar	
½ cup granulated sugar	1 Tbsp orange liqueur

★ Heat the oil in a Dutch oven. Brown the bird on all sides. Cover the breast with the strips of bacon.

★ Pour the wine over the bird. Cover and bake at 325°F for one hour, basting frequently with pan juices and turning twice during last half hour.

★ Combine brown sugar, granulated sugar and cornstarch in a saucepan. Add the orange rind, juice, salt and pepper. Simmer, stirring until thick.

★ Add the orange liqueur and continue stirring for 2 minutes. Serve the duck and coat with the sauce at the table.

Wild Duck

BRAZOS DUCK   Serves 2

2 ducks
⅓ stick butter per duck
   salt and pepper

1 tsp thyme
1 tsp sweet basil
1 tsp oregano
2 Tbsp Worcestershire sauce
1 pinch red pepper

¼ cup Burgundy wine
1 onion, chopped
1 can consommé
1 can beef bouillon   or 2 cups game stock
   freshly ground black pepper
4 stalks chopped celery
1 chopped green pepper

2 oranges

★ Place ⅓ stick butter in each duck cavity. Sprinkle the birds well with salt and pepper. Place in a baking dish.

★ Mix all ingredients except oranges and pour over the ducks.

★ In a preheated 350°F oven, roast uncovered ducks for 2 hours, basting frequently.

★ Squeeze the juice from the oranges. Chop up the rind and add to the juice. Pour the juice and rind over the ducks. Cover and cook for ½ hour more.

★ During the last 20 minutes of cooking, increase to 400°F.

CANETON CAMPAGNE   Serves 4

A Recipe for the Electric Slow Cooker.

Rouen, on the Seine between Paris and the English Channel, is the home of the French duckling industry, and it was near Châlons-sur-Marne, on the Marne River south of Reims, that we were introduced to Caneton Campagne. We think you will be pleasantly surprised with this recipe converted to the electric slow cooker.

2   ducks, disjointed
1   tsp salt
½   tsp freshly ground black pepper

2   Tbsp butter

8   oz. cooked ham, sliced julienne
6   small white onions
2   leeks, sliced

1   carrot, sliced
1   clove garlic, minced

1½   cups Chablis wine
1   cup chicken broth

12   oz. frozen peas
½   pound fresh mushrooms, sliced
½   pound sliced green beans, blanched
2   medium potatoes, cubed

★ Wash and dry the duck pieces. Rub with salt and pepper.

★ Melt the butter in a skillet and brown the duck pieces on all sides.

★ Add the ham, onions, leeks, carrot and garlic.

★ Set the cooker on HIGH, add and stir in the duck, vegetables and ham..

★ Warm the wine and broth in a sauce pan. Add to the mixture in the cooker, cover and cook for 45 minutes at LOW setting.

★ Add the peas, mushrooms, blanched beans and potatoes. Cover and cook for 2 hours.

Wild Duck

DUCK À LA JACK   Serves 2 to 4

3 pounds duck pieces
well-salted water

2 Tbsp butter

2 Tbsp all-purpose flour
1 cup game stock or chicken stock
¼ cup Pouilly wine

1 cup fresh, sliced mushrooms
2 Tbsp chopped onion
½ bay leaf
½ tsp salt
freshly ground black pepper

thin slices of orange
snipped parsley

★ In a small amount of well-salted water, simmer the duck pieces for 20 minutes. Remove and drain the pieces.

★ Melt the butter in a heavy skillet and brown the duck pieces. Transfer to a 2-quart casserole.

★ Blend the flour into the pan liquids. Cook and stir until bubbling. Blend in the remaining ingredients except for the orange slices and parsley. Simmer and stir for a few minutes.

★ Pour the sauce over the duck pieces. Cover and bake at 350°F for 1½ hours.

★ Transfer the duck to a heated platter. Sprinkle with snipped parsley and lay a slice of orange on each piece.

★ Remove the bay leaf from the sauce. Skim off any excess fat. Serve the sauce in a gravyboat.

★ Serve the duck on a bed of wild rice. Spoon the sauce over the duck.

RIVER DUCK ARMAGNAC **Serves 2**

Perhaps some of you have found that Coot (Mud Hen, Whitebill, etc.) can be a game gourmet's delight. Once you have tried this recipe using breast of Coot you will stop calling it Mud Hen and start calling it Water Chicken.

2 duck or Coot breasts
salt
freshly ground black pepper

3 Tbsp butter
¼ cup Armagnac

¾ cup chicken stock
⅓ cup Rhine wine
2 Tbsp honey
¼ tsp ground cinnamon
2 cups cherries, pitted

★ Season the cavity of the ducks with salt and pepper and truss them. Roast in a preheated 350°F oven for about 1 hour (flesh must be slightly underdone).
(If using breast of Coot, lightly season with salt and pepper and roast for 30 minutes).

★ Cut the duck into serving pieces Melt the butter in a large skillet, add the duck pieces and turn them lightly in butter. Add the Armagnac and flame.

★ Add the chicken stock, wine, honey and cinnamon. Bring to the boiling point and add the cherries. Cover and simmer for 10 minutes.

★ Transfer the duck pieces to a heated platter. Spoon the cherries and hot sauce over the meat and serve.

Wild Duck

MADEIRA DUCK Serves 2

A Ragout

2 wild ducks with livers
salt
freshly ground black pepper

2 Tbsp butter
2 Tbsp safflower oil

1 onion, finely chopped
3 shallots, finely chopped
1 carrot, finely chopped
1 Tbsp butter
1 Tbsp safflower oil

1½ cups Chablis wine
3 Tbsp Madeira wine
1½ cups water
1 sprig parsley
½ tsp dried thyme
½ bay leaf

2 Tbsp butter
2 Tbsp flour

2 slices sourdough bread,
fried in butter

★ Season duck cavities with salt and pepper. Truss the birds. Mince and reserve the livers.

★ In a casserole, heat 2 Tbsp butter and 2 Tbsp oil. Brown the birds on all sides. Cover and cook over low heat for 30 minutes.

★ Carve the still rare meat from the ducks. Chop up the carcasses. Return the meat and carcasses to the casserole. Add the onion, shallots and carrot. Add 1 Tbsp butter and 1 Tbsp saffoil. Stir and cook until the meat is golden.

★ Mix together the Chablis, Madeira and 1½ cups water. Add to the cooking meat. Season with salt and pepper. Add the parsley, thyme and bay leaf. Cook, uncovered, over high heat for 30 minutes. ▶

★ Heat 2 Tbsp butter in a separate casserole. When the butter begins to turn brown, stir in the flour and cook while stirring until brown. Strain the pan juices from the duck, reserving the meat and discarding the bones. Stir the pan juices into the butter roux. Blend and simmer for 15 minutes.

★ Add the minced duck livers and the sliced duck meat to the sauce. Simmer slowly for 10 minutes. Serve on a hot platter, garnished with the fried bread.

DUCK À LA ORANGE   Serves 2

2 ducks, halved lengthwise
salt
freshly ground black pepper

Glaze:
2 Tbsp butter

1 onion sliced and separated into rings
2 Tbsp orange juice concentrate
1 Tbsp fresh lemon juice
2 Tbsp honey
½ tsp ground ginger
¼ tsp ground allspice

★ Salt and pepper the duck halves. Place on a rack in a shallow roasting pan. Tent with aluminum foil. Roast in a preheated 400°F oven for 1 hour or until tender.

★ Glaze for Basting. While the duck is browning, melt the butter in a saucepan and sauté the onion rings until tender, but not brown. Stir in the orange juice, lemon juice, honey, ginger and allspice. Heat just to the boil.

★ During the last ten minutes of roasting, skim off the excess fat and baste the duck with the glaze.

Wild Duck

ROAST DUCK WITH SAUCE MOUTARDE Per serving

1 2-pound wild duck
   salt
   freshly ground black pepper
   thin sheets of pork fat

½ cup melted butter

   duck's liver
1 Tbsp butter

2 shallots, finely chopped

1 Tbsp butter
1 cup rosé wine
1 Tbsp Armagnac brandy

   juice of ½ lemon
1 tsp grated lemon peel
1 tsp prepared Dijon mustard
2 Tbsp parsley, chopped
   salt
   freshly ground black pepper

★ Season the bird's cavity with salt and pepper. Place the bird breast-up on a trivet in a roasting pan. Lard the breast with the thin sheets of pork fat.

★ In a preheated 450°F oven, roast the bird for 30 minutes, basting frequently with melted butter.

★ While the duck is roasting, sauté the liver in 1 Tbsp butter for 5 minutes.

★ Remove the liver and purée in a blender. In the same sauce pan, sauté the shallots with additional Tbsp butter. Add the wine and brandy. Bring to a boil.

★ Lower the heat and add the duck liver purée, lemon juice, grated lemon peel, Dijon mustard and parsley. Salt and pepper to taste.

★ Transfer the duck to a heated platter. Add the pan juices to the mustard sauce and serve in a gravyboat. Carve the duck and spoon the sauce over the meat.

40

TRABEN-TRABACH ENTE   Serves 3 to 6

A recipe from the Moselle River valley of Germany converted to the American electric slow cooker.

2 ducks, cut into eating pieces	1 pinch ground thyme
2 cups Claret wine	½ tsp salt
½ cup brandy	½ tsp freshly ground black pepper
1 Tbsp Kirsch liqueur	½ bay leaf
2 onions, chopped	
1 clove garlic, minced	¼ cup vegetable oil
	½ pound fresh mushrooms, sliced

★ Wash the duck pieces and dry on paper towels. Place in a deep bowl.

★ Mix all ingredients, except mushrooms and oil, and pour over the duck. Marinate for 12 hours.

★ Heat the oil in a skillet and brown the duck pieces on all sides.

★ Set the cooker on HIGH and transfer the duck to the pot. Pour the marinade over the duck. Cover and cook for 2 hours.

★ Uncover, add the mushrooms, reducing heat to LOW. Cover and cook for 45 minutes or until tender.

Wild Duck

STUFFING FOR DUCK, HUNTER STYLE

1 duck's liver, chopped
⅔ cup fresh sourdough bread crumbs,
     moistened with milk
1 onion, chopped
½ clove garlic, minced
½ tsp dried thyme

½ tsp dried savory
1 tsp dried rosemary

salt
freshly ground black pepper
brandy

★ Combine with duck's liver, bread crumbs, onion, garlic and herbs.

★ Season with salt and pepper and sprinkle with brandy.

★ Cover and refrigerate for 1 hour.

Wild Goose

Wild Goose

There is an old German saying that "one goose is too much for one man to eat yet not enough to feed two."

Geese have been a part of international cuisine for over 3,000 years, and every schoolboy remembers that a flock of geese warned the Romans of the approaching Gauls in 390 B.C.

Because wild geese live primarily on fish their flesh generally carries that flavor. This flavor can be removed by first carefully cleaning the bird, plucking it and stuffing the cavity with a mixture of chopped onion and lemon. This mixture is left in the cavity for twenty-four hours and then discarded. Another excellent method for removing the fishy taste is to soak the goose overnight in milk before preparing for the oven.

BRAISED BRANDT   Serves 4

1 wild goose	¼ cup lean pork, finely chopped
salt	1 tsp parsley, chopped
freshly ground black pepper	1 bay leaf
¼ tsp nutmeg	1 large pinch ground thyme
1 tart apple, peeled, cored and sliced	1 whole clove
3 slices bacon, blanched	1 clove garlic, mashed
	salt and pepper
Sauce	1 Tbsp dark rum
2 Tbsp butter	½ cup game stock
1 carrot, chopped	1 tsp paprika
1 onion, finely chopped	

★ Clean and singe the goose. Season the cavity with salt, pepper and a dash of nutmeg. Place the apple in the cavity. Bard with the bacon slices.

★ Place the goose in an earthenware pot or Dutch oven. Cover tightly and bake at 450°F for 35 minutes.

★ While the goose is baking, make the sauce:

Melt the butter in a saucepan. Sauté the carrot, onion, chopped pork, parsley, bay leaf, thyme, clove and garlic for 10 minutes. Season with salt and pepper. Add the rum and game stock. Simmer for 10 minutes, seasoning with paprika.

★ Add the sauce to the goose. Remove the bacon and cook for an additional 30 minutes.

Wild Goose

CHESTNUT GOOSE   Serves 8

8 pounds goose pieces
2 Tbsp butter
2 Tbsp peanut oil
1 garlic clove, mashed
2 onions, minced
4 carrots, minced
1 stalk celery, minced

1 cup game stock
1 cup dry white Rhine wine

2 Tbsp tomato purée
  boiling water
1 herb sack (1 sprig parsley,
    1 sprig thyme, 1 bay leaf,
    ½ tsp rosemary leaves)
  salt
  freshly ground white pepper

1½ pounds chestnut meat.

★ Use choice goose pieces.

★ Heat the oil and butter in a large casserole. Lightly sauté the garlic, onions, carrots and celery. Add the goose pieces and sauté until golden on all sides.

★ Add the game stock, wine, tomato purée, and just enough water to cover the goose pieces. Add the herb sack, season with salt and pepper, cover and simmer over low heat for 2 hours.

★ Remove the herb bag. Add the chestnut meat, cover and simmer for 40 minutes more.

★ Transfer the goose meat to a heated serving dish, and the chestnuts to a heated bowl. Serve with the pan juices spooned over the goose and chestnuts.

REAL GONE GOOSE   Serves 2 to 4

1 adult wild goose
1 cup dry bread cubes
1 cup cooked prunes, pitted and
  quartered
4 tart apples, peeled, cored and
  quartered
¼ cup yellow raisins
½ cup chopped celery

½ tsp salt
  freshly ground black pepper
¼ tsp ground sage
¼ tsp dried rosemary, crushed
¼ tsp MSG (optional)
  thin sheets of pork fat

★ In a large bowl, toss together all ingredients.

★ Stuff and truss the geese, with the sheets of pork fat over the breast. Place the birds on a trivet in a shallow roasting pan.

★ In a preheated 400°F oven, roast and baste the birds with pan drippings until tender.

Wild Goose

ROAST GOOSE WITH SAUERKRAUT   Serves 2

1 wild goose
    salt and pepper
    juice of 1 lemon

6 cups drained sauerkraut
2 tsp caraway seeds
2 strips chopped bacon

1 Tbsp honey
1   tsp MSG (optional)

4 slices blanched bacon

1 cup game stock

★ Preheat oven to 325°F.

★ Salt and pepper the cavity. Sprinkle lemon juice inside and out.

★ Combine all ingredients of the stuffing. Fill the body cavity, truss the bird and place it breast side up on a trivet in a shallow roasting pan.

★ Cover the breast with the blanched bacon strips. Soak a large piece of cheesecloth in melted bacon fat and cover the breast and bacon with it.

★ Roast the goose for 1 hour. Add the game stock, cover and cook for 1 more hour.

Partridge and Woodcock

Partridge and Woodcock

Partridge and woodcock are found in many parts of America, and are called by many names. Quail and grouse are sometimes referred to as partridge, but whatever the name, they are delicious.

The few partridge recipes provided here were designed for French partridge, but we have used them for Blue Grouse and Drummer Partridge for many years.

PARTRIDGE IN WHITE SAUCE   Serves 4

4   partridge (game hens, woodcock
      or similar sized birds)

2   slices bacon, chopped
      oil

3   Tbsp clarified butter

¼   cup chopped mushrooms
4   Tbsp flour
3   cups game stock or chicken broth
2   sprigs parsley
4   green onions, chopped
¼   tsp thyme
1   bay leaf
      salt
1   whole clove

4   peppercorns

12 small onions
½   tsp salt
¼   tsp sugar

2   tsp fresh lemon juice
¼   cup water
½   cup mushroom caps

4   egg yolks
1   cup heavy cream
1   Tbsp cherry brandy

      salt
      freshly ground pepper

★ Blanch the bacon in boiling water. Fry in a little oil and reserve.

★ Combine 3 Tbsp of the bacon fat with the clarified butter in a large Dutch oven. Brown the birds on all sides. Remove the birds.

★ Add the mushrooms and sauté for 2 minutes. Stir in the flour and game stock, stirring until smooth. Add the parsley, green onions, thyme, bay leaf, salt, clove, and peppercorns.▶

Partridge and Woodcock

★ Return the birds to the pot. Cover and braise for 30 minutes.

★ In a saucepan, cook the onions with salt and sugar until tender. Drain and reserve.

★ Combine the lemon juice and water, add to the saucepan. Cook the mushroom caps until tender. Reserve for topping.

★ Transfer the birds to a heated, deep platter. Surround with the reserved onions.

★ Strain the sauce from the Dutch oven into a saucepan and stir in the combined egg yolks and cream. Cook over very low heat, adding the brandy a bit at a time until thickened. Let just bubble, but do not boil.

★ Salt and pepper the sauce to taste. Pour over the birds, topping with the reserved mushroom caps. Serve at once.

MINTED PARTRIDGE   Serves 2

4 partridge breasts, skinned and boned	2 Tbsp lemon juice
4 hard-boiled eggs, diced	1 egg, slightly beaten
2 Tbsp chopped fresh mint	4 slices bacon, chopped
salt	¼ cup white game stock, heated
white pepper	¼ cup butter
¼ tsp ginger	
¼ tsp nutmeg	

▶

★ Pound the breasts of the birds with the back of a knife to flatten. Form into similar shapes.

★ Mix the boiled eggs, mint, seasoning, lemon juice and beaten egg together.

★ Put equal portions of the chopped bacon on each breast. Spread each with the egg mixture, rounding on all sides. Place in a baking dish.

★ Mix the game stock and margarine together. Pour one-half this mixture over the breasts.

★ Cover the dish with aluminum foil. Bake in a preheated 350°F oven, basting with the pan juices every 10 to 15 minutes, adding additional game stock and butter mixture as needed.

★ Bake for 45 minutes. Remove the foil and brown to a delicate golden color. Test with a knife for tenderness. Taste for seasoning. Serve from the hot baking dish.

TENDER TIMBERDOODLES   Serves 4

A fine way to keep game birds moist and tender is through slow steaming. All you need is a trivet in a Dutch oven which will keep the birds above the liquid level.

4 woodcock	2 Tbsp honey
2 tsp salt	1 Tbsp steak sauce
½ cup butter	1 cup mushrooms, quartered
½ cup boiling water	all-purpose flour
½ cup dry sherry	½ tsp paprika

▶

Partridge and Woodcock

★ Carefully clean the birds until squeaky clean. Rub lightly with salt. Place the birds on a trivet in a Dutch oven, over medium heat.

★ Mix the butter and boiling water. Pour over the birds, cover and steam for 1 hour.

★ Mix the sherry with the honey in a warm saucepan. Add the meat sauce and mushrooms.

★ Pour the sherry mixture over the birds. Sprinkle lightly with flour. Cover and steam for 1 to 1½ hours. Test with fork for tenderness.

★ Remove the birds. Sprinkle lightly with paprika and keep warm.

★ Remove the trivet. Stir the sauce and thicken with a little flour if too thin. Serve the sauce in a gravyboat for spooning over the birds on toasted English muffins or toast wedges.

Pheasant

Pheasant

Pheasant can be a dish fit for a king or can taste like an army surplus knapsack boiled in gall. Pheasant should never be fried like chicken as this is a guarantee that you'll wind up with the above mentioned knapsack.

My favorite recipe is PHEASANT CASSEROLE, in which the birds are cut into eating pieces, seasoned, browned and cooked in a Dutch oven with links of smoked sausage. We have enjoyed this dish in hunting camps across the nation, wherever the glorious Chinese Ringneck graces our fields of grain.

BASIC ROAST PHEASANT   Serves 2 to 4

1	pheasant	3	eggs, beaten
	salt	¼	cup evaporated milk
	pepper		
			butter
1	onion, chopped		flour
1	cup crisp cabbage, chopped	3	strips bacon

★ Pluck and draw the pheasant. Season the cavity with salt and pepper.

★ In a mixing bowl, beat and mix the onion and cabbage until well mixed. Blend in the 3 lightly beaten eggs. Add and blend in the evaporated milk. Stuff the bird with the mixture and sew the cavity closed.

★ Rub the bird with butter and flour. Cover the breast with strips of bacon.

★ Preheat the oven to 325°F. Bake the pheasant for about one hour, covered.

★ Uncover, remove the bacon and cook for an additional 15 minutes to brown the breast.

Pheasant

BALLOTINE OF PHEASANT   Serves 6 at buffet

This recipe is a bit more complicated than some of the others, but well worth the effort. It is a superb dish for a buffet dinner.

1 pheasant	1 veal bone
salt and pepper	1 onion, stuck with 2 whole cloves
⅓ cup chopped mushrooms	1 carrot
6 Tbsp butter	2 cloves garlic
3 ounces ground pork	6 peppercorns
3 ounces foie gras	1 herb sack (1 sprig parsley, ½ bay
salt	leaf, 1 branch thyme, 1 sprig
3 truffles, chopped	rosemary)
water	1 truffle, sliced

★ Bone the pheasant. Lay skin side down on a large cloth. Lightly salt and pepper. Reserve the carcass.

★ Sauté the mushrooms lightly in butter. Mix with the pork, foie gras and salt.

★ Spread the mixture over the pheasant and sprinkle with the chopped truffles.

★ Roll the pheasant and cloth lengthwise into a firm roll. Wrap the cloth tightly around the roll and tie at intervals of 4-6 inches. Securely tie the ends.

★ Place the roll in a large kettle. Cover with water and add the veal bone, pheasant carcass, onion, ▶

carrot, garlic, peppercorns and herb sack. Cover, bring to a boil and simmer for 1 hour.

★ Remove the pheasant roll from the kettle and let cool. Remove the cloth. Refrigerate for 2 hours. Discard the herb sack.

★ Reduce six cups of the kettle liquids to three. Season to taste. Strain the liquids through a damp cheesecloth, let cool, then refrigerate for aspic.

★ Slice the pheasant roll in ½ inch slices. Coat with aspic and top with a slice of truffle.

JAEGER CHEF PHEASANT   **Serves 4**

1   pheasant, quartered

1½ cups game stock
1   cup apple cider
1   Tbsp Worcestershire sauce
¾   tsp salt

⅓   cup chopped onion
1   clove garlic, minced
1   cup sliced mushrooms

paprika

★ Preheat oven to 350°F. Place the pheasant in a baking dish 10″ x 2″ deep.

★ Mix all ingredients except paprika. Pour the mixture over the bird.

★ Bake for 1 hour, uncovered, spooning off the excess fat. Baste once or twice with pan juices.

★ Sprinkle with paprika and bake for an additional 30 minutes.

Pheasant

BRANDIED PHEASANT   Serves 4

1 pheasant
   thin sheets of fresh pork fat
   salt
   freshly ground black pepper

½ cup fresh butter

¼ cup brandy
¼ cup sherry

½ cup game stock

★ Dress and clean the bird. Wrap in the sheets of pork fat and tie securely while trussing. Season with salt and pepper.

★ Melt 4 Tbsp of the butter in a casserole. Over high heat, brown the bird until golden on all sides.

★ Cover the casserole and simmer for 45 minutes over low heat.

★ Take the bird from the casserole and remove the pork fat. Skim off the fat from the pan juice. Return the bird to the casserole. Add the brandy. Flame. Add the sherry, cover the casserole and simmer for 10 minutes.

★ Transfer the pheasant to a heated platter.

★ Add the game stock to the pan juices. Bring to a boil and cook for a few minutes. Stir in the remaining butter and blend. Pour the sauce over the bird and serve.

MOIST PHEASANT IN SOUR CREAM SAUCE AND WINE   Serves 4

1 pheasant, skinned and cut into serving pieces
½ tsp salt
½ cup all-purpose flour
½ tsp freshly ground black pepper
½ tsp celery salt
  milk
4 Tbsp butter

½ cup game stock or chicken broth
2 green onions, cut in ½" lengths
½ cup sliced celery
1 orange peel, cut julienne
1 cup dry white wine
1 Tbsp honey
1 cup mushroom caps
1 cup sour cream

★ In a paper bag, combine the salt, flour, pepper and celery salt. Dip the pheasant pieces in a bowl of milk, drop into the paper bag and shake to coat.

★ Melt the butter in a skillet. Over medium heat, brown the pieces on all sides. Transfer the pieces to a Dutch oven and keep warm.

★ Blend some of the flour mixture with the butter remaining in the skillet until a thick paste is formed. Add the game stock, onions, celery and orange peel. Stir and cook for 3 minutes.

★ Mix the wine with the honey. Add to the sauce.

★ Pour the sauce over the pheasant in the Dutch oven. Cover and bake for 2 hours at 325°F.

★ Mix the mushroom caps with the sour cream. Add to the pheasant, stir in, cover and cook for an additional 30 to 40 minutes.

★ Serve hot over a bed of wild rice.

Pheasant

PHEASANT FANTASY   Serves 6

2 pheasant

3 Tbsp butter
2 slices bacon, chopped
2 carrots, diced
2 onions, diced
2 stalks celery, diced
2 Tbsp Madeira

2 cups Chablis
2 cups game stock
¼ tsp thyme
1 bay leaf

   salt and pepper

Sauce

½ cup chopped mushrooms
5 Tbsp butter
5 Tbsp all-purpose flour
1½ cups game stock (reserved from
      first part of recipe)
2 tsp lemon juice
1 Tbsp cherry brandy
¼ tsp nutmeg

2 egg yolks
4 Tbsp heavy cream

1 cup bread crumbs
2 ounces Parmesan cheese, grated
   butter

★ Clean and truss the birds.

★ Heat the butter in a large kettle. Lightly brown the bacon, carrots, onions and celery. Add the Madeira and cook for 2 minutes more.

★ Add the pheasant to the kettle. Add the wine, stock, thyme and bay leaf. Cover and simmer for 1½ hours. ▶

★ Remove the pheasant. Let cool and remove the trussing twine.

★ Reduce the stock in the kettle to 1½ cups. Salt and pepper to taste. Strain and reserve for the sauce.

★ Now, make the sauce:

In a sauce pan, sauté the mushrooms in butter for 2 minutes. Stir in the flour and blend until smooth. Add the reserved 1½ cups of game stock, lemon juice, brandy and nutmeg. Cook, stirring continuously, until satin smooth.

In a separate bowl, mix together the egg yolks and cream. Very gradually beat in ½ cup of the hot game stock sauce. Return the mixture to the sauce pan, beating continuously. Reheat, but do not let boil. Strain and discard the mushrooms.

★ Let the sauce cool while you place the pheasant in a shallow casserole. Spoon the cooled sauce over the pheasant, entirely coating it.

★ Combine the bread crumbs and cheese. Sprinkle over the pheasant. Dot with butter.

★ Place the casserole in a 375°F oven and bake until golden.

Pheasant

FRENCH PHEASANT   Serves 2 to 4

1 pheasant
   salt
   freshly ground black pepper
   thin sheets of pork fat
4 Tbsp sweet butter
¼ cup Calvados

2 dozen tiny white onions, browned
     in butter
½ pound fresh mushrooms, browned
     in butter
3 truffles, diced

★ Season the pheasant with salt and pepper. Wrap in the fresh pork fat and truss it. In a casserole, brown on all sides in the butter.

★ Reduce the heat, pour the Calvados over the bird, cover and simmer for 45 minutes.

★ Remove the pork fat. Add the onions, mushrooms and truffles. Heat for five minutes, then serve.

PHEASANT IN SOUR CREAM   Serves 2 to 4

1 pheasant
4 strips fat bacon

4 Tbsp butter
   salt
   freshly ground black pepper

1 pound tart apples, peeled and sliced

1 cup sour cream
¼ cup dry white wine (recommend a
     Moselle)

¼ cup Calvados ▶

★ Truss the pheasant. Lay the bacon strips across the breast and secure with twine.

★ Heat the butter in a casserole and brown the pheasant on all sides. Season with salt and pepper.

★ Reduce the heat, cover and simmer for 30 minutes. Add the apples and cook until golden.

★ Add the sour cream and wine. Simmer, covered, for 20 minutes more.

★ Remove the bacon, re-cover and cook for another 5 minutes.

★ Remove the casserole from the heat. Pour the Calvados over the bird and serve hot from the casserole.

SPANISH PHEASANT   Serves 2

1 pheasant

⅔ cups coarsely chopped mushrooms

3 cups port wine

2 Tbsp peanut oil

½ cup minced onion

4 chicken livers, chopped

1 pheasant liver, chopped

3 Tbsp parsley, chopped
   salt and pepper

3 slices bacon, blanched

★ In a large sauce pan, simmer the mushrooms in port wine for about 10 minutes. Strain and reserve the mushrooms. Let the wine cool, saving for marinade.

★ In a skillet, heat the peanut oil and sauté the minced onion. Remove the onion and reserve. Sauté the livers for 10 minutes. Purée the livers in a blender. ▶

Pheasant

★ Mix the puréed livers with the parsley, and reserved mushrooms and onion. Season to taste with salt and pepper. Fill the cavity with the mixture. Close with skewers and truss the bird. Refrigerate for six hours, basting with the wine marinade at least 4 times.

★ Place the pheasant on a rack in a shallow baking pan. Cover the breast with the blanched bacon. Pour the wine marinade over the bird.

★ In a preheated 350°F oven, roast for 1 hour, basting frequently with the pan juices.

★ Remove the bacon. Continue cooking until the breast is browned and the bird is tender.

★ Transfer the pheasant to a heated platter. Reduce the marinade to ½, skimming off any excess fat. Serve the wine sauce in a gravyboat for spooning over the pheasant.

PHEASANT CASSEROLE   Serves 3 to 4

2 cock pheasant, properly hung	2 Tbsp butter
½ cup all-purpose flour	½ pound smoked sausage links
1 tsp ground sage	
salt and pepper	½ cup butter
1 pinch curry powder	6 Tbsp all-purpose flour
	4 cups fresh milk
2 Tbsp bacon fat	

★ Clean the pheasant and cut into eating pieces. Mix the flour, sage, salt, pepper, and curry powder in a paper bag. Coat the pieces of pheasant by shaking them in the paper bag mixture. ▶

★ Heat 2 Tbsp bacon fat and 2 Tbsp butter in a skillet. Brown the pheasant pieces on all sides.

★ Transfer the pheasant to a heated Dutch oven. Top with the links of smoked sausage.

★ In a separate skillet, melt the ½ cup butter and thicken it with 6 Tbsp all-purpose flour. Add the 4 cups milk, blending in.

★ Bring to a slow boil, stirring briskly. Pour over the pheasant and sausage. Bake in a preheated oven very slowly (250°F) for 2 hours.

PHEASANT SALAD   Serves 4

1½ cups cooked pheasant meat, cut into small cubes

¼ cup salad oil
1 Tbsp fresh orange juice
1 Tbsp fresh lemon juice
1 clove garlic, crushed

¼ tsp salt
½ tsp freshly ground black pepper

4 seedless oranges, peeled and sectioned
1 onion, thinly sliced
4 Tbsp fresh mint, chopped

fresh spinach leaves

★ In a bottle, blend the oil, fresh fruit juices and seasoning. Shake well.
★ In a large bowl, mix together the cubed pheasant, orange sections, onions and mint.
★ Pour just enough salad dressing over the pheasant mixture to coat well. Toss lightly.
★ Chill for one hour. Line a salad bowl with fresh spinach leaves. Spoon the pheasant mixture over the spinach leaves and serve.

Quail

Quail

There are several varieties of quail, the best known in America being the bobwhite. Its name is derived from its clear, piercing call which sounds like a young girl calling to Bob White with the last name a rising, shrill note.

Young quail can be broiled, roasted, panfried or panbroiled. Adult birds are best when cooked in a Dutch oven and the older birds best when done in a cream sauce or marinade. Smoked quail is a real delicacy and any of your favorite smoking woods will smoke them well.

Quail, like dove, should be cleaned immediately in the field and the gall bladder carefully removed so that spoilage of the delicately flavored flesh is prevented.

BUTTER CREAM QUAIL   Serves 4

12 quail
1 pound fresh sweet butter
1 pint heavy cream

salt
freshly ground black pepper
1 Tbsp honey

★ Slowly melt the butter in a heavy iron skillet. Add the quail. Spoon the butter over them until they are golden brown and the butter is greatly reduced.

★ Add the heavy cream. Cook slowly, basting frequently until tender. Season with salt and pepper to taste.

★ Stir in the honey during the last few bastings.

★ Serve on a bed of hot hominy.

CHARCOAL GRILLED QUAIL SHERRY   Serves 2 hunters or 4 dainty eaters

8 quail
½ cup honey
1 tsp curry powder
1 cup sherry

3 tsp cinnamon
1 tsp garlic salt
½ tsp celery salt

★ Place the quail in a shallow baking dish. Blend all ingredients and pour over the quail. Marinate overnight in the refrigerator. ▶

71

Quail

★ Drain and save the marinade.

★ Using a charcoal broiler with enough depth so that the grate is at least four inches above the charcoal, wait until the charcoal is covered with a good white ash. Place the quail on the grill breast up.

★ Baste with the reserved marinade, turning every 5 minutes. Cook slowly for about 1 hour or until done (quail will be dark brown when done).

BOBWHITE REWARD   Serves 3 to 4

6 quail	1 tsp sage
2 lemons	1 tsp salt
¼ pound butter	1 cup dry white wine
½ cup olive oil	
1 clove garlic, crushed	

★ Place the quail in a shallow roasting pan. Squeeze the juice of 1 of the 2 lemons over the birds.

★ Melt the butter and mix with the olive oil. Rub the quail with the crushed garlic and brush with the butter and oil mixture.

★ Sprinkle the birds with sage and salt. Cut second lemon into thin strips. Add these and the juice to the wine. Pour the mixture over the birds.

★ Cover and roast in a preheated 325°F oven for 1 hour or until tender. Remove the cover and brown. Serve hot over hot slices of toast.

QUAIL WITH LENTILS   **Serves 4**

8 quail or grouse	6 shallots, chopped
2 cups dry lentils	2 herb sacks (parsley, rosemary, thyme, peppercorns, sliver of garlic)
salt	
freshly ground black pepper	1 cup Pouilly wine (or any dry white wine)
8 thin sheets pork fat for barding	
4 Tbsp butter	1 cup game stock
2 carrots, chopped	2 cups onions, chopped

★ Soak the lentils overnight in cold water.

★ Season the cavities with salt and pepper. Wrap the breasts with barding fat and secure with cooking twine. Truss the legs and wings.

★ Melt the butter in a large casserole. Add the birds and brown evenly over medium high heat.

★ Add the carrots, shallots and 1 herb sack. Combine the wine and game stock and pour over the birds. Cover and simmer slowly for 1½ hours.

★ Drain the soaked lentils and place them in a large saucepan. Cover with cold water. Add the remaining herb sack and onions. Bring to a boil. Reduce heat, cover and simmer for 40 minutes. Drain and keep hot.

★ Transfer the birds to a heated serving platter. Strain the casserole liquids and spoon over the birds. Surround the birds with the lentils and serve hot.

Quail

BUTTERMILK QUAIL   Serves 4 to 6

12 quail
1 pint buttermilk

1½ cups self-rising flour
1 tsp grated lemon rind

salt
freshly ground black pepper

2 cups safflower oil

★ Place the dressed birds in a large bowl. Pour the buttermilk over them and let soak for 1 hour.

★ Combine the flour, lemon rind, salt and pepper in a large bowl. Roll the birds in the mixture.

★ Heat the oil in a deep skillet. Test for correct temperature by dropping small balls of flour and water mixture in the oil. The flour balls will sizzle like doughnuts when the oil is ready.

★ Fry the quail in the hot oil until golden brown.

BBQ QUAIL   Per serving

2 quail

1 Tbsp peanut oil
3 Tbsp butter

½ bay leaf
thin sheets of fresh pork fat

salt
freshly ground black pepper

1 cup bread crumbs

½ cup game stock ▶

★ Split the birds along the breastbone and flatten them.

★ Heat the oil and butter in a casserole. Brown the birds.

★ Add the bay leaf, cover the breasts with the pork fat, season with salt and pepper and simmer for about 5 minutes.

★ Remove the birds. Dip them in the bread crumbs.

★ Charcoal broil the birds for 3 to 4 minutes on each side. Transfer them to a hot platter.

★ Add the game stock to the casserole and bring to a boil. Immediately remove the sauce. Serve in a sauceboat.

QUAIL CASSEROLE   Serves 4

6 quail	salt and pepper
1 Tbsp butter	½ tsp savory
salt	2 Tbsp butter
3 strips bacon	1 cup game stock
3 slices sourdough bread	

★ Skin the quail, rub with butter and salt. Wrap each with ½ strip bacon.

★ Dice the bread. Mix well with salt and pepper, savory and 2 Tbsp butter. Stuff the birds with this mixture.

★ Place birds in a casserole. Pour game stock over them and bake at 350°F for 1½ hours.

Quail

CAMPFIRE QUAIL #1   Serves 2 to 4

6 quail

½ cup peanut oil

1 pinch each:
   salt
   freshly ground black pepper

onion powder
basil
thyme
rosemary

lemon juice

★ Mix the oil with the seasonings. Rub the birds with this mixture.

★ Place a grill over a bed of hot, gray coals. Broil birds quickly for about 10 minutes or until tender, basting frequently with the remaining oil mixture.

★ Transfer the birds to a hot platter. Sprinkle with the lemon juice.

★ Serve on a slice of hot, buttered sourdough French bread.

CAMPFIRE QUAIL #2   Serves 2

4 quail
   salt
   freshly ground black pepper

½ cup boiling water
½ cup melted butter

2 Tbsp steak sauce
1 cup chopped mushrooms
½ cup dry sherry
   flour

   paprika ▶

★ Carefully clean and pluck the birds. Rub lightly with salt and pepper.

★ Place the birds in a Dutch oven. Mix the hot water and butter. Pour over the birds, cover and steam for 30 minutes.

★ Add the steak sauce, chopped fresh mushrooms and sherry. Dust lightly with flour. Steam for 40 minutes.

★ Remove the birds to a heated platter. Sprinkle lightly with paprika and serve.

HUNTERS' QUAIL   Serves 2

4 quail	½ bay leaf, crushed
salt	½ tsp dried thyme
freshly ground black pepper	½ cup game stock
5 Tbsp butter	½ cup Rhine wine
1 Tbsp flour	

★ Using whole quail, season with salt and pepper. Tie the legs and wings to the bodies.

★ Melt the butter in a casserole or Dutch oven. Sauté the birds until golden. Sprinkle with flour and brown on all sides for 1 minute more.

★ Reduce heat. Add the bay leaf, thyme, game stock and wine. Simmer, covered, for 15 minutes.

★ Place the birds on a heated platter and pour the pan sauce over all.

Quail

BOBETTE'S BIRDS   Serves 3

6 quail, skinned
½ tsp salt
   butter

3 slices sourdough bread
¼ tsp freshly ground black pepper
½ tsp savory
   pinch rosemary

1 Tbsp butter
1 small can mushroom caps

3 strips lean bacon

1 Tbsp butter
⅓ cup dry white wine

★ Rub each bird with salt and butter.

★ Lightly brown the bread and cut into small pieces. Hand mix with pepper, savory, rosemary, butter and brine from the mushrooms, reserving the mushroom caps.

★ Stuff the birds and wrap each with ½ strip bacon across the breast.

★ Over low heat, melt 1 Tbsp butter in a Dutch oven. Add the birds, pour the wine over the birds, cover and cook for 2 hours.

★ Uncover and add the mushrooms. Cover and cook for an additional 20 minutes.

VARIATION #1: Bake, covered, in a 350°F oven for 1 hour and 30 minutes.
VARIATION #2: Mix the mushroom caps (or ½ cup chestnut meat instead of mushrooms) into the stuffing.

Quail

GOPHER GUS' GASTRONOMIQUE   Serves 3 to 4

6 quail, skinned and split
   down the back
1 cup all-purpose flour
4 Tbsp butter

1 large can sauerkraut

½ tsp salt
½ tsp freshly ground black pepper

½ can beer
1 twig wild sage (if available)

★ Wash and drain the birds. Dredge in flour. Melt the butter in a skillet and brown the birds lightly. Remove and reserve the birds.

★ Drain the sauerkraut and place in a Dutch oven over medium heat. Place the birds on the bed of sauerkraut. Pour the butter remaining in the skillet over the birds. Lightly sprinkle with salt and pepper.

★ Pour the beer over the birds and lay the twig of sage on top. Cover and cook for 4 hours or until tender.

★ Remove the birds and sauerkraut. Thicken the pan liquids with a little flour and serve.

Quail

QUAIL CARAMEL Serves 2

4 quail

1 cup sugar

4 Tbsp butter

1 cup game stock

1 Tbsp flour

½ cup cream

1 tsp dry sherry
   Worcestershire sauce
   salt
   freshly ground black pepper

★ Preheat oven to 325°F.

★ In a heavy skillet, make a caramel of the sugar.

★ Place the birds in an open roasting pan and sprinkle with the caramel.

★ Place 1 Tbsp butter on the breast of each bird. Add the game stock and roast for 1 hour, basting frequently.

★ Remove the birds to a bed of hot brown rice and keep hot.

★ Blend the flour and cream and stir into the pan juices. Add the sherry and a few drops of Worcestershire sauce. Season to taste with salt and pepper.

★ Spoon the sauce over the birds and serve.

QUAIL MUSCAT   **Serves 2**

4 quail (or Chukar partridge)	¼ cup cognac, warmed
6 Tbsp butter	1 tsp orange liqueur
4 thin sheets pork fat for barding (or blanched bacon)	4 slices sourdough French bread, fried in butter
6 dozen Muscat seedless green grapes salt freshly ground black pepper	

★ Rub the birds with a little of the butter. Wrap with the pork fat and truss.

★ Heat the remaining butter in a casserole. Add the birds and brown on all sides over medium high heat for 15 minutes.

★ Reduce the heat to moderate and add the grapes, salt and pepper. Cover and cook for 15 to 20 minutes until tender.

★ Remove the birds and untruss. Discard the pork fat.

★ Mix the warmed cognac and orange liqueur. Return the birds to the casserole, sprinkle with the cognac mixture and flambe.

★ Transfer the birds to a heated serving platter. Garnish with the grapes and fried bread. Pour the pan juices over all and serve.

Quail

SMOTHERED QUAIL   Serves 4

4-6 quail
    milk

1 tsp salt
1 tsp pepper
½ cup all-purpose flour

½ cup peanut oil

½ cup game stock

¾ cup dry white wine

4 stalks celery, with leaves
1 cup mushroom caps

    orange juice concentrate

★ Soak the quail in milk for several hours.

★ Mix the salt, pepper and flour in a paper bag. Dust the birds by shaking them in the paper bag. Reserve flour for making the roux.

★ Heat the peanut oil in a heavy skillet. Brown the quail in the oil. Transfer the birds to an earthenware casserole.

★ Make a light brown roux of the skillet drippings, adding the game stock.

★ Add the wine and stir in. Pour the mixture over the quail.

★ Chop the celery stalks and leaves, placing over the birds. Add the mushroom caps, cover and bake for 1½ hours at 325°F.

★ Serve over wild rice. Sprinkle with orange juice concentrate.

QUAIL IN WHITE WINE   Serves 3 to 4

6 quail
salt
flour

4 Tbsp butter

½ cup minced onion

½ cup minced mushrooms
1 Tbsp parsley
½ cup dry white wine

½ cup heavy cream

★ Pluck and draw the birds. Rub with salt and flour.

★ Melt the butter in a casserole or Dutch oven and lightly sauté the birds.

★ Sauté the onion, mushrooms and parsley in a skillet. Add the wine. Pour over the birds.

★ Simmer for 30 minutes, basting frequently. Add the heavy cream. Heat thoroughly and serve over wild rice.

GROUSE CALVADOS   Per serving

1 grouse
salt
freshly ground black pepper

1 stick butter

1 large green apple, cored and minced

3 Tbsp heavy cream
4 Tbsp Calvados

1 Tbsp crushed strawberries
(optional) ▶

Quail

★ Season the bird with salt and pepper. Truss the bird.

★ Melt ½ the stick of butter in a heavy skillet. Over brisk heat, brown the bird until golden.

★ Remove the bird from the heat. Split down the back into two parts.

★ Heat the remaining ½ stick butter in a casserole. Sauté the apple until golden.

★ Place the bird halves on the sautéed apple. Sprinkle with Calvados and heavy cream. Cover and cook in a 350°F oven for 35 minutes.

★ Uncover the bird, sprinkle with crushed strawberries (optional) and serve.

IRISH GROUSE   Serves 2

2 grouse	1½ cups game stock
1 head cabbage	½ cup safflower oil
salt	2 onions, finely chopped
freshly ground black pepper	2 carrots, finely chopped
¾ cup Chablis or dry Riesling wine	¼ pound bacon, chopped
	1 herb sack (1 bay leaf, 1 sprig thyme, 2 sprigs parsley, 1 sprig rosemary)

★ Cut the cabbage into quarters and blanch in boiling salted water for a few minutes. Remove with a slotted spoon, drop into cold water, then drain in a sieve. Reserve.

★ Truss the birds, rub with salt and pepper and place in a buttered baking pan. In a preheated ▶

450°F oven, roast for 10 minutes. Turn until golden on all sides. Transfer the birds to a heated and covered platter. Keep warm.

★ Stir the wine and game stock into the roasting pan, scraping up all drippings and mixing well.

★ In a large casserole, heat the oil. Add the vegetables and bacon. Mix well and cook until golden. Add the reserved cabbage and herb sack. Season with salt and pepper. Pour the pan juice over the cabbage, cover and cook over medium heat for 1 hour. Stir occasionally. Add the birds and spoon the vegetables over them. Cook for an additional 15 minutes, then serve hot.

SCOTCH GROUSE   Per serving

1 grouse	½ cup chopped celery
pork fat for barding	½ cup chopped onion
5 Tbsp butter	¼ cup brandy
salt	¼ cup Scotch
freshly ground black pepper	½ cup game stock
½ cup chopped carrots	

★ Clean, pluck and truss the bird. Wrap it in thin sheets of pork fat.

★ Heat the butter in a baking pan and brown the bird. Season with salt and pepper. Remove from the heat and sprinkle the vegetables around and over the bird.

★ In a preheated 450°F oven, roast the bird for ten minutes. Reduce temperature to 350°F and roast ▶

until tender (30 to 40 minutes). Remove the pork fat and brown the breast at 400°F, basting frequently.

★ Transfer the bird to a heated platter.

★ Skim the fat off the pan juices. Return the bird to the pan. Mix in the brandy and Scotch. Flambé the bird. Add the game stock.

★ Cover the pan. Return to the oven and let simmer for 5 minutes.

★ Transfer the bird to a bed of wild rice. Pour the pan sauce over the bird and serve at once.

BLUE GROUSE BETINA   **Serves 2 to 4**

4 grouse	¾ cup port wine
salt	
freshly ground black pepper	8 slices sourdough French bread
6 Tbsp safflower oil	
6 Tbsp butter	

★ Season the cavities with salt and pepper. Truss the birds.

★ Heat half the oil and half the butter in a very large casserole. Brown the birds on all sides.

★ Remove the birds. Cut the breast away from the rest of the bird and then cut the breast in half, ▶ providing 8 pieces of breast meat and breast bone.

★ Reserve the carcasses for making game stock and soup.

★ Pour the oil and butter out of the casserole. Add the port wine and scrape up the pan drippings.

★ Return the breasts to the casserole. Season with salt. Bring to a boil then reduce and simmer, covered, until tender (about 15 minutes).

★ Fry the bread slices in the remaining oil and butter.

★ Serve the breasts hot over the fried bread slices. Spoon the pan sauces over the birds.

STUFFING FOR QUAIL
(2 birds)

1/8 pound finely ground pork	salt
1/8 pound finely ground ham	cayenne pepper
1/8 pound ground veal	2 Tbsp brandy

Rabbit

Rabbit

While chicken is an important part of every diet and menu, we feel that Brer Rabbit has been ignored by too many for too long. Rabbit is plentiful almost anywhere in America and many hunters were initiated into the society of hunters as young boys on their first rabbit hunt.

There are parts of Europe where entire cuisines are built around rabbit and hare. If you want to get "Old Timers" moist-eyed, just start talking about an early morning rabbit hunt and different ways to cook rabbit - you'll learn how important rabbit is in America.

One problem with being a cook par excellence of rabbit is that you will probably be the camp chef during all hunting trips.

While Hase means hare, you aren't likely to find the Belgian Hare in your lettuce patch, but Hasenpfeffer can be prepared equally well with either domesticated or wild rabbit.

A BIT OF THE HARE   Serves 4 to 6

Seems this feller, Nimrod, went quail hunting after promising several friends a quail dinner. He didn't have much luck and every time he looked back along his trail he saw this rabbit following him. With few quail in his bag, he finally took aim and dropped brer hare. As the appointed hour approached, Nimrod knew he'd be short at least two quail, so told his wife to cook the rabbit. Guests seated and candles lit, Frau Nimrod carried in the heaping platter.

"And of what, my dear, will you partake?" she asked Nimrod.

"Oh, I think I'll just have a bit of the hare that dogged me," he said.

2 **rabbits, quartered**	2 **Tbsp butter**
3 **cups water**	3 **slices bacon, diced**
½ **cup dry white wine**	1 **Tbsp sugar**
½ **cup cider vinegar**	3 **Tbsp Kirsch liqueur**
1 **Tbsp salt**	
2 **Tbsp allspice**	3 **Tbsp all-purpose flour**
1 **Bermuda onion, sliced**	3 **ginger snaps, crumbled**
1 **carrot sliced**	½ **cup sour cream**

★ Wash the rabbits in cold water. Remove excess skin and rinse again. Dry on paper towels.

★ Prepare the marinade of the water, wine, vinegar, seasonings, onion and carrot. Pour the marinade over the rabbit in a crockery jar or glass bowl. Refrigerate for 48 hours.

★ Remove the rabbit from the marinade. Dry on paper towels. Strain the marinade and reserve. ▶

Rabbit

★ Melt the butter in a skillet and brown the bacon. Transfer the bacon to a Dutch oven or casserole and add ½ cup marinade.

★ Brown the rabbit on all sides. Transfer the rabbit to the casserole with the bacon and marinade. In a preheated 325°F oven, cover and cook for 1 hour.

★ Mix the sugar and Kirsch liqueur. Pour over the rabbit, cover and cook for 1 hour longer.

★ Combine the flour, 1 cup marinade and the crumbled gingersnaps. Stir into the casserole liquid, cover and cook for 1 hour longer.

★ Uncover and stir in the sour cream. Reduce the oven temperature to 300°F, cover and cook for 30 minutes.

★ Transfer the rabbit to a heated platter. Spoon the sauce over the meat and serve.

BELGIAN RABBIT Serves 2 to 4

1	plump rabbit	3 Tbsp Dijon mustard
	salt	1 Tbsp chopped fresh thyme
	pepper	
		thin sheets of fresh pork fat

★ Preheat oven to 450°F.

★ Season the cavity with salt and pepper. Spread the cavity with Dijon mustard and sprinkle with ▶ thyme.

★ Wrap the rabbit in thin sheets of fresh pork fat (or you can use fat bacon). Tie with kitchen twine. Place on a trivet in a shallow roasting pan.

★ Roast in the preheated oven for 15 minutes. Reduce the heat to 350°F and roast for 45 minutes longer, turning and basting with pan liquids.

★ Remove the pork fat and let brown for 30 minutes or until done.

BAVARIAN RABBIT   Serves 4

2 pounds choice rabbit pieces

3 smoked pork sausages
½ cup dry red wine
½ cup beer

¼ cup apple cider vinegar
1 cup clear game stock or consommé

1 cup browned bread crumbs
1 tsp caraway seeds
½ lemon peel, grated
1 tsp brown sugar
    salt
    freshly ground black pepper

★ Parboil and drain the rabbit pieces.

★ Place the pork sausage in a Dutch oven or large skillet and cover it with the wine and beer. Cover and simmer for 30 minutes.

★ Remove the sausage and skim off the fat. Add the rabbit, cider vinegar, game stock, browned bread crumbs, caraway seeds, lemon peel and brown sugar. Season with salt and pepper to taste.

★ Stir well, cover and simmer gently for 2 hours. Return the sausage to the mixture, heat for a few minutes and serve.

Rabbit

MISSION RABBIT   Serves 4
A Recipe for the Electric Slow Cooker

1   medium rabbit, cut up
1   cup dry white wine
½   cup Beaujolais wine
1   clove garlic, peeled
1   clove garlic, minced
½   tsp dried thyme
½   tsp dried sweet basil
½   tsp salt

¼   tsp freshly ground black pepper
1   stick butter
12   small garden carrots
12   cocktail onions, rinsed
1   small jar stuffed olives

★ Mix wine, garlic, thyme, basil, salt and pepper for a marinade. Marinate the rabbit for 24 hours, turning once.

★ Drain rabbit pieces. Dry on paper towels. Remove garlic from the marinade. Reserve the marinade.

★ Melt the butter in a skillet. Brown the rabbit.

★ Set slow cooker on HIGH. Transfer rabbit and butter to slow cooker.

★ Add marinade, carrots and onions. Cover and cook for 3 hours.

★ Uncover, add the olives, cover and cook for 15 minutes.

★ Remove rabbit from liquids and serve. Pour liquids into a gravyboat and serve with the rabbit.▶

VARIATION #1: Add chopped rind of ½ lemon to marinade.
VARIATION #2: Add 1 Tbsp Kirsch liqueur when adding olives.
VARIATION #3: Add ¼ pound sliced mushrooms with the olives.

OLD COUNTRY HASENPFEFFER   Serves 4

2 adult rabbits, quartered	½ tsp basil
4 cups apple cider vinegar	2 tsp salt
4 cups water	½ tsp freshly ground black pepper
2 onions, sliced	
4 whole cloves	4 Tbsp butter
1 bay leaf	1½ cups thick dairy sour cream

★ In a large crock, mix the vinegar, water, onions, cloves, bay leaf, basil, salt and pepper. Add the rabbit pieces. Marinate for two days.

★ Remove the rabbit. Strain the marinade and reserve 1½ cups.

★ Melt the butter in a large skillet. Brown the rabbit until dark golden brown on all sides. Add the reserved marinade gradually, lower the heat and let simmer slowly for 30 minutes.

★ Remove the rabbit and keep heated. Stir the sour cream into the pan juices and return the rabbit to the sauce. Heat well and serve.

Rabbit

DAD'S RABBIT   Serves 4

2 adult rabbits, quartered
4 cups apple cider vinegar
4 cups water
2 onions, sliced
4 whole cloves
1 bay leaf
½ tsp basil
2 tsp salt
½ tsp freshly ground black pepper

1 stick butter

2 onions, sliced
2 Tbsp all-purpose flour
4 carrots, sliced
1 bay leaf
1 pinch curry powder
1 large pinch ground sage
2 cups dry red wine
   butter and flour for a roux
1 tsp lemon juice
1 tsp steak sauce

★ Marinate the rabbit as in OLD COUNTRY HASENPFEFFER.

★ In a Dutch oven, melt the butter and sauté the sliced onions. Sprinkle with 2 Tbsp flour and stir until brown.

★ Add the rabbit and cook until the meat is evenly browned.

★ Add the carrots, bay leaf, curry powder and sage. Stir well. Add the wine, cover and cook over very low heat for 40 minutes.

★ Remove the rabbit pieces. Make a roux with a little flour and butter. Add the lemon juice and steak sauce, stirring into the pot liquor. Return the rabbit and heat while the sauce thickens.

★ Taste for seasoning and serve.

Rabbit

JACK'S RABBIT   Serves 6

3½ pounds choice rabbit pieces
buttermilk
2   tsp salt

5   Tbsp butter

1   medium sized onion, sliced
3   whole cloves
1   cup port wine
¼   cup cider vinegar

¼   cup lemon juice
20   ounces condensed beef broth
1   herb sack (½ tsp dried thyme leaves,
      8 peppercorns, 1 sprig parsley,
      1 bay leaf)

3   Tbsp butter
3   Tbsp all-purpose flour

★ Marinate the rabbit pieces overnight in buttermilk. Rinse and dry the rabbit pieces. Rub with salt.

★ Melt the butter in a skillet. Sauté the rabbit until golden on all sides.

★ In a Dutch oven over low heat, combine the onion, cloves, port wine, vinegar and lemon juice. Add the beef broth and herb sack.

★ Transfer the rabbit to the Dutch oven. Cover and cook for 2 hours.

★ Uncover. Discard the onion and herb sack.

★ Melt 2 Tbsp butter in a saucepan over low heat. Stir in 3 Tbsp flour until smooth. Stir in about 3 cups of stock from the Dutch oven, bring to a simmer and stir until thickened. Taste for seasoning.

★ Transfer the rabbit to a heated serving platter. Pour the sauce over the rabbit and serve.

Rabbit

JO'S RABBIT   Serves 4

1   rabbit, cut into eating pieces
1   Tbsp lard
½ pound pork, cut into small cubes

1   tsp salt
1   tsp freshly ground black pepper
1   cup beer

1   medium onion, chopped
1   carrot, sliced
1   potato, sliced
4   stalks celery, sliced

2   Tbsp flour

★ Melt the lard in a skillet. Sear the rabbit and pork on all sides over high heat.

★ Transfer the rabbit and pork to a Dutch oven. Salt and pepper to taste. Add the beer and stir for a few seconds over medium heat.

★ Add the vegetables, stir and cover. Cook for two hours over low heat.

★ Remove the cooked meat. Mix 2 Tbsp flour with ¼ cup liquid from the pot. Stir and return to the pot. Cover and cook until the liquids have thickened, stirring occasionally.

★ Pour the sauce over the rabbit and pork and serve hot.

RABBIT MARQUETTE   Serves 6 to 8

4   pounds choice rabbit parts

2   Tbsp safflower oil
4   Tbsp butter
2   dozen tiny white onions
½   pound bacon, cut in thin strips

    salt
    freshly ground black pepper

¼   cup brandy

1   bottle dry white wine
1   Tbsp honey
4   Tbsp flour
2   cloves garlic, mashed
1   herb sack (1 sprig parsley, ½ bay leaf, 1 sprig thyme or 1 tsp dried thyme)

1   cup mushroom caps

★ Heat 1 of the 2 Tbsp oil and 2 of the 4 Tbsp butter in a casserole. Sauté the onions until light gold. Add the bacon strips and stir until the bacon becomes transparent. Remove the onions and bacon and reserve.

★ Brown the rabbit pieces on all sides, seasoning with salt and pepper.

★ Sprinkle with brandy. Flambé, being careful when you ignite the brandy.

★ Heat the wine and honey in a saucepan. Sprinkle the flour over the rabbit and add the heated wine, garlic and herb sack. Cover and simmer over low heat for 45 minutes.

★ Sauté the mushroom caps in the remaining 1 Tbsp oil, 2 Tbsp butter and a little salt. Reserve.

★ When the rabbit has finished cooking, discard the herb sack. Add the reserved onions, bacon and mushrooms. Stir and then transfer all to a heated platter.

Rabbit

TURNIP PATCH RABBIT   Serves 4

1 rabbit, quartered	1 bay leaf
Dijon mustard	2 tsp sugar
1 onion, stuck with 4 cloves	6 fresh, tender turnips
dry white wine	4 Tbsp butter
1 stick butter	½ cup dry white wine
2 Tbsp olive oil	
salt	1 Tbsp chopped parsley
freshly ground black pepper	tarragon
1 tsp thyme	

★ Coat the rabbit pieces with Dijon mustard. Place in a large glass bowl with the onion and enough wine to cover. Refrigerate for 24 hours.

★ Melt 1 stick of butter in a large skillet. Add the olive oil. Drain the rabbit, reserving the marinade. Brown on all sides. Remove to a casserole and season with salt, pepper and thyme. Add the bay leaf. Sprinkle with 2 tsp. sugar.

★ Strain the marinade and pour over the rabbit. Cover and cook in a preheated 350°F oven for 1 hour.

★ While the rabbit is cooking, peel the turnips and brown them in a skillet with 4 Tbsp butter. Turn until evenly browned. Cover and gently steam until just tender.

★ Transfer the rabbit to a heated platter and surround with the turnips. Strain the sauce from the ▶

turnips and add ½ cup wine. Bring to a boil, then quickly reduce.

★ If the sauce is too thin, make a roux with flour and butter to thicken. Sprinkle the sauce with parsley and tarragon. Pass the sauce in a sauceboat.

SMOTHERED RABBIT   Serves 4

3 pounds rabbit legs and saddles	salt
2 Tbsp safflower oil	pepper
4 Tbsp butter	
	3 Tbsp Dijon mustard
1 onion, stuck with 2 cloves	½ cup thick cream
1 herb sack (1 clove crushed garlic,	1 pinch cayenne pepper
1 sprig parsley, 1 bay leaf, 1 Tbsp	2 egg yolks, beaten
celery leaves, 1 sprig thyme or 1	1 Tbsp fresh lemon juice
tsp dried thyme)	

★ Heat the oil and butter in a Dutch oven over medium-high heat. Brown the rabbit pieces evenly on all sides.

★ Reduce the heat. Add the onion, herb sack, salt and pepper. Cover and simmer for 30 minutes.

★ Discard the onion and herb sack. Blend the mustard with the cream, add the cayenne, egg yolks and lemon juice. Pour over the rabbit. Simmer very slowly until the sauce has thickened. Taste for seasoning and serve.

Rabbit

SPITTED RABBIT   Serves 2

1   plump, tender rabbit
1   onion, sliced
1   carrot, sliced
1   sprig thyme
2   bay leaves
1   sprig parsley

freshly ground black pepper
1   tsp salt
1   cup wine vinegar

¼   pound fat bacon strips

★ Skin and clean a tender, plump rabbit.

★ In an earthenware crock, mix all ingredients except the bacon strips. Marinate the rabbit for 24 hours, turning once.

★ Drain and dry the rabbit. Lay the strips of fat bacon across the chest and back and over the legs, trussing the rabbit with twine to hold the bacon in place.

★ Skewer the rabbit and roast over a bed of coals for 45 minutes or until tender.

Rabbit

SAUTÉED RABBIT   Serves 4 to 6

3 pounds choice rabbit parts	freshly ground black pepper
8 Tbsp peanut oil	¾ cup rosé wine
6 Tbsp olive oil	2 garlic cloves, minced
1 pound small mushroom caps	2 Tbsp parsley, minced
3 green onions, minced	3 slices sourdough bread, cubed
salt	

★ Heat 4 Tbsp of the peanut oil and 4 Tbsp of the olive oil in a Dutch oven or heavy skillet. Brown the rabbit parts until golden on all sides. Lower the heat, cover and simmer for 25 minutes. Remove the rabbit pieces and keep warm.

★ Sauté the mushroom caps in the pan juices. Add the green onions. Season with salt and pepper. Remove and keep warm.

★ Return the rabbit to the pot, add the wine and season with a little salt and pepper. Cover and simmer for 15 minutes. Add the garlic and parsley.

★ Remove the rabbit, place in a deep serving dish, pour the pan juices over it and top with the mushrooms and onions.

★ In a heavy skillet place the 4 Tbsp peanut oil and 2 Tbsp olive oil. Fry the bread cubes until crisp and golden. Sprinkle over the rabbit and serve.

Venison

Venison

Venison represents literally thousands of tons of prime meat taken each year across our land. Unfortunately, much of it is wasted through spoilage and as much, or more, through improper cooking.

In the colder areas hunters have learned to clean and hang the animal immediately after the kill. Later, the animal is skinned and the exposed meat wiped clean of all hair and blood.

Venison is best if hung for two or more weeks in a cool place, just a few degrees above freezing. The carcass is then butchered and wrapped for freezing, the choice cuts going directly to the kitchen.

We have an annual ritual of making venison sausage. This sausage is a crowd-pleaser at all festive buffets throughout the year, as well as a vital part of every hunter's breakfast when returning to the high country.

Deer, elk, moose, caribou . . . all are venison and all can be delicious if prepared properly. We would rather have saddle of antelope in sour cream sauce than any cut of beef in any kind of sauce, and we think you will too.

Many hunters fail to get the most out of large game. Estimates suggest that from 40% to 74% of all downed game is ruined by poor field–dressing, butchering and/or bad care of the meat. Another 10-20% is wasted because hunters don't know how to use and prepare all the parts. We are talking about a lot of wasted prime meat.

The electric slow cooker will reduce much of this waste. We have included in this section several recipes for less-often prepared parts of venison. While these recipes are for the Dutch oven, they can be converted to the slow cooker by reducing 30-35% of the liquid and slightly decreasing the seasoning measurements.

VENISON CASSEROLE   Serves 6 to 8

4 pounds venison, cut in 2" cubes
2 cups Beaujolais wine
½ cup fresh lemon juice
1 onion, sliced
1 carrot, sliced
1 clove garlic, minced
1 bay leaf
¼ tsp thyme
½ tsp tarragon

2 tsp salt
½ tsp freshly gound black pepper

4 Tbsp butter
¼ pound fresh mushrooms, sliced
12 small white onions

½ pound chicken livers
1 Tbsp minced shallots
2 Tbsp butter

★ In a glass bowl, mix the wine, lemon juice, onion, carrot, garlic, bay leaf, thyme, tarragon, salt and pepper. Add the meat and marinate for two days, turning 4 times. Drain well, strain and reserve the marinade.

★ In a large skillet, brown the meat in 4 Tbsp butter. Add the mushrooms and small white onions. Sauté for 5 minutes.

★ Pour off the fat. Transfer the meat, onions, mushrooms and 1 cup of marinade to a casserole. Cover and bake in a 350°F oven for 1½ hours.

★ 15 minutes before done, sauté the chicken livers and shallots in 2 Tbsp butter. Stir into the casserole mixture. Taste for seasoning.

★ Serve with thick slices of sourdough bread.

Venison

VENISON STEAK, HUNTER STYLE   Serves 3 to 4
Dutch Oven for Camp or Home

6 venison fillet steaks, cut about
    ⅓" thick
all-purpose flour
salt
freshly ground black pepper

3 Tbsp peanut oil
2 large onions, sliced

2 cloves garlic, sliced
½ cup water

★ Season the flour with salt and pepper. Dredge the steaks.

★ Heat the oil in a Dutch oven. Lightly sauté the onion, remove and reserve.

★ In the same oil, brown the steaks on both sides. Return the onion, add the garlic and stir for two minutes. Add the water.

★ Cover and simmer for 30 minutes. Transfer to a heated platter.

★ Serve with hot apple sauce and steamed brown rice.

BROILED VENISON CHOPS   Serves 3

6 venison chops

½ cup peanut oil
¼ cup vinegar
1 tsp sugar

1 tsp lemon or lime juice
1 tsp salt
freshly ground white pepper   ▶

★ Mix the oil, vinegar, sugar, lemon juice, salt and pepper until well combined.

★ Place the chops in a baking dish. Pour the oil mixture over the chops and marinate for 2 to 3 hours.

★ Broil for 30 minutes, turning once.

BUCKBOARD VENISON   Serves 6 to 8

4 pounds venison, cut in 1" cubes
1 cup all-purpose flour
1 tsp salt
1 tsp freshly ground black pepper

2 Tbsp peanut oil
1 pound fresh mushrooms, quartered
1 green pepper, minced

1 onion, chopped
¼ pound butter

1 can tomatoes
3 cups game stock

1½ cups Beaujolais wine

★ Combine the flour, salt and pepper. Dredge the venison cubes.

★ In a Dutch oven or heavy iron pot, heat the peanut oil. Saute the mushrooms, green pepper and onion until lightly golden. Remove and reserve.

★ At higher heat, add the butter and melt. Sear the meat until well browned on all sides.

★ Return the sautéed vegetables to the pot with the venison. Add the tomatoes and enough game stock to cover. Simmer for 2 hours.

★ Add the wine. Bring to a boil, then lower heat to simmer for ½ hour longer.

Venison

TRINITY VENISON ROAST   Serves 4 at dinner (with leftovers for sandwiches)

5 pounds venison rump roast	3 whole allspice
2 cups vinegar	2 onions, sliced
2 cups water	2 celery tops
2 Tbsp brown sugar	1 sprig pine needles
3 tsp salt	
½ tsp freshly ground black pepper	1 cup all-purpose flour
½ lemon peel, cut julienne	4 Tbsp lard
3 whole peppercorns	
1 clove garlic	4 Tbsp raisins
1 bay leaf	
5 whole cloves	6 gingersnaps

★ Mix the vinegar, water, sugar, salt, pepper, lemon peel and spices. In a large pan, boil the marinade mixture for 5 minutes. Let cool.

★ Place the roast in a large glass bowl or crock. Pour the cooled liquids over the roast. Place onion slices and celery tops over the meat and the pine sprig over all. Cover and refrigerate for 3 days, turning the meat daily.

★ Remove the meat from the marinade and drain well. Strain the liquids and reserve.

★ Dredge the roast in flour. In a Dutch oven, melt the lard and brown the roast on all sides.

★ Lower the heat to medium. Add 1 cup marinade and 4 Tbsp raisins. Cover and cook for 4 hours. ▶

★ Remove the roast to a heated platter. Crumble the gingersnaps and add to the pot liquid. Cook and stir occasionally for 15 minutes.

★ Slice the venison. Pour sauce from the pot into a gravyboat and spoon it over the sliced venison.

FOIE DE CHEVREUIL   Serves 4

2	pounds cured venison liver	1	bay leaf
1	tsp kosher salt	3	sprigs parsley
1	cup boiling water	¼	tsp ground thyme
		¼	tsp ground black pepper
¼	cup all-purpose flour	1	onion, sliced
1	Tbsp lard	½	cup Rhine wine

★ Rub the liver with kosher salt and place in a large glass bowl. Pour boiling water over the liver and let stand for 5 minutes.

★ Drain the liver, reserving the water. Dry the liver and dredge with half the flour.

★ Melt the lard in a Dutch oven. Brown the liver. Add the herbs, pepper, onion, wine and ½ of the reserved water. Cover and cook slowly for 2 hours.

★ Remove and slice the liver. Keep warm on a heated platter.

★ Thicken the pot liquids with 2 Tbsp of the remaining flour and 3 Tbsp additional white wine. Pour the sauce over the liver and serve.

Venison

VENISON RAGOUT #1   Serves 6

You can use the neck and other lean parts for this camp stew, cutting them into bite-sized morsels and dredging them in seasoned flour in a paper bag. They are heavenly for lunch or dinner.

3	pounds venison parts	4	potatoes, quartered
1	cup all-purpose flour		
	salt		salt
	pepper		pepper
		½	tsp thyme
2	Tbsp lard	½	tsp celery salt
		½	tsp rosemary
2	onions, sliced or quartered	½	tsp minced parsley
1	clove minced garlic	½	cup dry white wine
1	cup diced celery		
1	can small white onions	2	Tbsp dark rum

★ Combine the flour, salt and pepper in a paper bag. Dredge the venison pieces in the flour by shaking in the bag.

★ Melt the lard in a Dutch oven. Brown the venison on all sides and reserve.

★ In the lard remaining in the Dutch oven, sauté the sliced onions and garlic until just golden. Return the venison and stir in the vegetables.

★ Add the salt, pepper, thyme, celery salt and rosemary. Sprinkle with parsley and add the wine. Cover and cook for two hours in preheated 325°F oven.

★ Uncover, add the rum, stir until blended and serve hot.

Venison

VENISON RAGOUT #2   Serves 8

3 pounds venison shoulder,
   cut in ½" cubes
   boiling water
1 bouquet garni (tie in cheesecloth sack:
      4 whole cloves
      6 crushed peppercorns
      1 slice of ginger root
      1 small cinnamon stick
      2 sprigs parsley
      2 Tbsp celery leaves
      1 clove garlic, crushed)

1 clove garlic, minced
5 potatoes, quartered
½ cup celery, diced
1 cup onions, diced
1 cup carrots, diced
   salt

   all-purpose flour
   butter

1 cup fresh peas
2 Tbsp lemon juice
1 Tbsp chopped parsley

★ Place venison in a large pot. Cover with boiling water and add bouquet garni. Simmer for 25 minutes.

★ Remove the bouquet garni. Add minced garlic, potatoes, celery, onions, carrots and salt to taste. Cover and cook over low heat for 45 minutes or until vegetables are tender.

★ Pour off the stock and measure. For each cup of stock, add a roux of 1 Tbsp flour and 1 Tbsp butter. Cook and stir until thickened into a sauce.

★ Add the peas to the sauce and cook for 5 minutes. Stir in the lemon juice and parsley. Pour the sauce over the cooked meat and vegetables. Serve hot.

113

Venison

ROAST VENISON AND SOUR CREAM   Serves 4
Dutch Oven Style

2 pounds venison
3 carrots
4 stalks celery

salt
freshly ground black pepper

3 cups rosé wine
2 Tbsp all-purpose flour
2 Tbsp butter
hot water
1 pint sour cream

★ Cut venison in ¾" x 3" pieces. Split the carrots and cut each strip in half. Cut the celery stalks into 3" pieces.

★ Salt and pepper the meat. Combine with the carrots and celery.

★ Place the venison and vegetables in a Dutch oven. Add the rosé wine, cover and cook for 2 hours at 350°F.

★ In a large skillet, make a roux of the flour and butter, cooking until lightly brown. Add a little hot water and then the sour cream. Stir until smooth.

★ Transfer the venison, carrots and celery to the skillet. Cover and simmer for 1 hour, adding small amounts of water if the sauce becomes too thick.

CURRIED VENISON   Serves 4

2 cups diced, cooked venison

½ tsp curry powder
1 Tbsp brandy

2 Tbsp butter
1 cup cooked lima beans

1 tsp finely minced onion
¼ tsp ground mace
¼ tsp white pepper
½ pound spinach, chopped

½ cup halved cashew nuts

★ Dissolve the curry powder in the brandy and combine with all remaining ingredients except the cashews.

★ Pour the ingredients into a covered baking dish or Dutch oven. Cook for 30 minutes in a preheated 350°F oven. Add the cashews and cook for an additional 15 minutes.

★ Serve over steaming rice.

VENISON SAUSAGE

4 pounds ground venison
6 pounds ground pork
3 ounces salt

1 ounce fresh ground black pepper
3 cloves garlic, mashed

★ Mix all ingredients well. Form into patties or stuff sausage skins.

Venison

VAGABOND VENISON Serves 4

1 deer heart
1 deer tongue

2 Tbsp lard or bacon grease
2 medium onions, sliced
1 tsp salt
1 tsp freshly ground black pepper

1 can mushroom caps
   with brine
2 Tbsp sherry
1 Tbsp dark rum

½ tsp paprika

★ Cut heart and tongue into bite sized pieces.

★ Melt the lard in a Dutch oven. Sauté the onions until golden. Add the heart and tongue and stir for a minute. Sprinkle with salt and pepper to taste.

★ Add the mushroom caps with brine, sherry and rum. Stir and cover. Cook over medium heat for 35 minutes. Reduce heat to low and cook for 2-3 hours until tender.

★ Sprinkle with paprika and serve hot over noodles.

VENISON CHUTNEY   Serves 2

2 cups sliced, cold cooked venison

¼ cup chopped chutney

1 cup left-over venison gravy

½ cup dry white wine

★ Mix the chutney, gravy and wine. Cover and cook in a sauce pan or chafing dish over medium heat until the mixture bubbles.

★ Uncover. Add and stir in the venison. Cover and cook for an additional 15 minutes.

★ Serve with hot wild or brown rice.

SMOKED VENISON ROAST   Serves 6
A Campfire Recipe

1 venison ham, boned

4 strips bacon

salt

pepper

★ Roll the bacon up and place in the bone cavity. Season the cavity with salt and pepper. Sew tightly closed.

★ Soak hickory or pecan chips for 1 hour (California oak bark is great). Build a good bed of coals in a smoker and when well ashed, place the venison on a grate over the coals. Smoke for 3 to 5 hours.

Venison

ANTELOPE À LA ROSÉ   Serves 6

3 pounds boneless shoulder, cut into
   bite sizes and trimmed of fat
   salt
1 tsp freshly ground black pepper

3 Tbsp olive oil
1 clove garlic, minced

1 cup rosé wine

1 Tbsp honey
½ tsp fresh rosemary
1 dash of hot pepper sauce

2 eggs
1 Tbsp freshly grated lemon rind

2 Tbsp rosé wine
1 Tbsp flour

★ Season the antelope meat with salt and pepper.

★ Heat the oil in a skillet and sauté the garlic until golden. Add the antelope pieces and brown on all sides over medium heat.

★ Transfer the meat to a Dutch oven.

★ Add the wine, honey, rosemary and hot pepper sauce. Cover and cook for 1½ hours.

★ Reduce the heat to low. Uncover the pot and drain off the broth, reserving it.

★ Beat the eggs in a bowl. Add 2 Tbsp broth and the grated lemon rind.

★ In a saucepan, over medium heat, heat the remaining broth.

★ Mix 2 Tbsp rosé wine with 2 Tbsp flour. Stir into the heated broth to thicken. Do not boil.

★ Add the egg and broth mixture to the heated broth and stir well. Spoon over the meat and serve.

118

ANTELOPE NECK WITH SOUR CREAM   **Serves 4**

2   **pounds antelope neck (young animal)**
¼   **cup all-purpose flour**
1   **tsp salt**
¼   **tsp black pepper**
1   **pinch tarragon**
1   **pinch thyme**
2   **Tbsp butter**

2   **bouillon cubes**
1   **cup boiling water**
1   **onion minced**
¼   **tsp caraway seeds**
2   **Tbsp lemon juice**
¼   **cup dry white wine**

★ Dredge the antelope neck in flour seasoned with salt, pepper, and herbs.

★ Melt the butter in a Dutch oven. Brown the neck.

★ Dissolve the bouillon in 1 cup boiling water. Add the remaining ingredients and pour over the neck. Cover and cook for 2 hours.

Venison

LORD GORE'S BROTH   Serves 4

In the late 1880's, England's Lord Gore led a safari of hunting gentlemen across northern Colorado. We came across the recipe attributed to him near Walden, Colorado, where the North Platte River dwindles away into Grizzly Creek.

2 pounds breast of antelope, cut up	3 onions, chopped
4 Tbsp butter	1 cup celery, sliced
	½ cup barley
1 antelope shank	1 package soup greens
3 cups water	1 cup carrots, diced
1 tsp salt	½ cup rutabaga, diced
8 peppercorns	

★ Melt the butter in a Dutch oven or heavy skillet. Brown the antelope pieces over medium heat.

★ Add the remaining ingredients. Cover and cook for 3 hours at a low simmer.

★ Remove the meat. Let the mixture cool and remove all bones.

★ Over medium heat, bring the liquids to a slow simmer. Return the meat to the broth and cook, covered, for 1 more hour.

NORTH PARK ANTELOPE STEAKS   Serves 4

4   antelope steaks, up to ¾" thick
2   Tbsp flour per steak
¼   tsp salt per steak
¼   tsp freshly ground black pepper per
    steak
½   tsp dry mustard per steak

2   Tbsp lard or cooking oil

1   cup dry white wine
2   small onions, sliced
1   cup chopped celery
1   pinch rosemary

2   Tbsp flour

★ Pound the steak with flour, salt, dry mustard and pepper.

★ Heat the oil in a Dutch oven. Brown the steaks lightly on all sides.

★ Layer the steaks in the Dutch oven. Add the wine, onions, celery and rosemary. Cover and cook for 1 hour over medium heat.

★ Remove the steaks and keep hot. Make a roux with 2 Tbsp flour and 4 Tbsp pot liquid. Return the roux to the pot and cook uncovered until reduced to the desired consistency.

★ Pour the sauce over the steaks and serve.

Venison

THE ELEGANT ELK   Serves 8

4½ pound rump roast

1 cup olive oil
3 small onions
1 clove garlic, minced

1 tsp crushed rosemary
1 tsp salt
1 tsp freshly ground black pepper

½ tsp celery salt

½ cup dry white wine
2 cans mushrooms (without brine)
1 can chopped ripe olives
1 can tomato juice
1 tsp powdered horseradish

★ Over medium heat in a Dutch oven, heat the oil and sauté the onions and garlic until tender and golden. Remove and reserve.

★ Rub the roast with crushed rosemary, salt, pepper and celery salt. Brown the roast in the oil remaining in the Dutch oven. Return the sautéed garlic and onions, cover and cook for 1 hour.

★ Uncover, add the wine, mushrooms, olives, tomato juice and horseradish. Cover and cook for 1½ hours for well done.

★ Transfer the roast to a heated platter and slice. Pour the pot liquor over the meat and serve.

Sauces

Sauces

To be a master game chef the hunter must complement his game dishes with sauces designed for enhancement and appeal, not for disguising and smothering the delicate flavors of wild game.

Many of the recipes in this section call for Sauce Espagnole, the source of some of the finest brown sauces; Bordelaise, Diable, Italienne, Madère, Pèrigueux, Piquante and Porto all start with Sauce Espagnole.

If you make this sauce in large quantities you can store it in the freezer until needed, thus greatly reducing the preparation time for many wild game recipes.

HUNTER'S SAUCE
For venison steaks, cutlets and roasts.
Volume: 2½ cups

6 Tbsp butter, softened
¼ pound mushrooms, minced
salt
1 Tbsp minced shallots

2 Tbsp flour

1 cup dry white wine
1 cup beef or venison gravy
1 Tbsp tomato paste

1 pinch each of:
celery seed

chervil
chives
tarragon
fennel
parsley
basil
rosemary
thyme
bay leaf
salt
¼ tsp freshly ground pepper

★ In a heavy saucepan, melt 2 Tbsp of the butter and gently sauté the mushrooms for 5 minutes. Season with salt, add the minced shallots, and continue cooking for 5 minutes. Remove from the heat and reserve.

★ Add 2 more Tbsp of the butter to the saucepan. Add the flour and stir over medium heat until golden.

★ Gradually add the wine, gravy and tomato paste. Stir with a wooden spoon and bring to a boil. Lower the heat and let cook for 10 minutes. ▶

Sauces

★ Just before serving, add the reserved mushrooms and shallots, and a pinch each of the herbs. Cook just long enough to heat through, but do not boil. Remove from the heat and swirl in the remaining butter. Season to taste with salt and pepper and serve.

SAUCE VELOUTÉ

For game birds.
Volume: 6 cups.

6	Tbsp butter	1	cup heavy cream
6	Tbsp all-purpose flour		salt
4	cups concentrated game stock		freshly ground white pepper
6	egg yolks		juice of 1 lemon (optional)

★ Prepare a white roux with butter and flour in a saucepan over medium heat.

★ Moisten the roux with a little of the stock, then gradually stir all of it into the roux. Let cook for about 10 minutes.

★ Blend the egg yolks with the cream. Remove the roux from the heat and stir the egg yolks and cream into the sauce. Return to heat and bring the mixture just to boiling, stirring constantly.

★ Remove the mixture from the heat. Season to taste with salt and pepper. Stir in the lemon juice if desired.

SAUCE BÉCHAMEL

Many of the great white sauces have Béchamel Sauce as their base, The Marquis de Béchamel, steward of Louis XIV, King of France, originated this sauce from which came the blond and white sauces Aurore, Bercy, Cardinal, Chaud-Froid, Mornay, Normande, Raifort and Véronique - the better known white sauces. Sauce Velouté, in its many variations, comprises the balance of white sauces.

For fish, pheasant and other fowl
Volume: 4 to 5 cups

4   cups milk
2   tsp salt
     freshly ground white pepper
     cayenne pepper
     grated nutmeg

1   bouquet garni (tie in cheese cloth
        sack: ½ tsp thyme, ½ bay leaf,
                  2 sprigs parsley, minced
½   cup butter
½   cup flour

★ In a large saucepan, bring the milk to a boil. Season with salt, pepper, cayenne, grated nutmeg and bouquet garni. Simmer for a few minutes.

★ Prepare a white roux with the butter and flour. Plunge the base of the roux saucepan into cold water. ▶

Sauces

★ Strain the milk through a fine sieve and immediately add to the white roux. Return the mixture to the fire.

★ Bring the mixture to a boil, stirring constantly, and let simmer for 10 minutes.

★ If the sauce is too thick, thin it slightly with additional milk heated in a saucepan.

SAUCE AURORE
For poached eggs, pheasant, game birds and trout or bass.
Volume: 1¼ cups

To 1 cup Sauce Béchamel, add ¼ cup tomato purée and 1 tsp paprika.

CHEESE SAUCE
For fish, vegetables and some meat dishes.
Volume: 3½ cups

Add ½ cup grated Gruyère or Cheddar cheese to 3 cups Sauce Béchamel.

SAUCE ESPAGNOLE
Volume: About 3 quarts

⅔ cup butter
½ cup diced carrot
½ cup diced onion
½ cup diced celery
¼ cup diced ham

2 quarts game stock
1 bouquet garni (tie in cheese cloth
   sack: 2 Tbsp minced parsley
     ½ tsp crumbled dried thyme

½ tsp crumbled dried
   marjoram
¼ tsp whole allspice
1 small garlic clove
½ bay leaf)

½ cup all-purpose flour

½ cup tomato purée
½ cup white wine
1 tsp salt

★ To make a "mirepoix," melt ¼ cup of the butter in a large saucepan and cook the diced carrot, onion, celery and ham until tender. Drain off the butter and reserve.

★ Add the mirepoix to the game stock. Add the bouquet garni and simmer for 2 hours.

★ Remove the bouquet garni and strain the liquid, pressing to extract juices from the herbs.

★ To the reserved butter, add enough additional butter to make ½ cup. Put it in a large saucepan and stir in the flour. Cook, stirring, until it browns slightly, making a roux. Cool a minute and then stir in the strained liquid. ▶

Sauces

★ Add the tomato purée, white wine and salt. Simmer for 2 hours, skimming as necessary. The sauce should be thick enough to lightly coat a spoon when done.

★ Cool. Pack in half-pint containers and freeze until needed.

SAUCE SUPRÊME
For pheasant, quail, antelope or delicate vegetables.
Volume: About 2½ cups.

5 Tbsp butter	½ bay leaf
2 Tbsp all-purpose flour	¼ cup creme fraîche or heavy cream
2 cups white stock	
1 small onion stuck with 1 whole clove	1 Tbsp fresh lemon juice

★ Make a roux with 2 Tbsp of the butter and flour. Gradually stir in the stock.

★ Add the onion with clove and bay leaf. Cook over low heat, stirring constantly until smooth and thickened.

★ Simmer for 10 minutes and then strain the sauce.

★ Stir in the remaining butter and cream. Beat in the lemon juice.

★ Serve hot.

SAUCE POIVRADE

While this sauce is a bit complicated, it is essential for wild game.

Volume: About 2½ cups

1 **Tbsp vegetable oil**	6 **peppercorns, crushed**
2 **Tbsp butter**	½ **cup wine vinegar**
1 **carrot, thinly sliced**	
1 **medium onion, thinly sliced**	1 **tsp flour**
2 **parsley sprigs**	1 **tsp cornstarch**
	½ **cup dry red wine**
1 **pound livers and giblets from**	2 **cups strong chicken stock**
game birds	**(or Sauce Espagnole)**
1 **garlic clove, crushed**	
salt	2 **Tbsp brandy or cognac**

★ In a saucepan, heat the oil and butter together. Add carrot, onion and parsley. Sauté until tender.

★ Add the livers and giblets. Sauté until golden.

★ Add the crushed garlic, pinch of salt, crushed peppercorns and vinegar. Simmer gently until the vinegar has evaporated.

★ Stir in the flour and cornstarch. Mix with a wooden spoon for two minutes.

★ Add the wine and chicken stock. Cover and simmer for 30 minutes. Thicken with a butter and flour roux if needed.

★ Strain into a gravyboat. Add the brandy and serve.

Sauces

SAUCE DIABLE
For grilled meats or any meat in which a hot sauce is desired.
Volume: 1½ cups

1 cup Sauce Espagnole
1 Tbsp prepared mustard
1 Tbsp Worcestershire sauce
1 dash hot pepper sauce (or Jalapeño sauce)

1 Tbsp vinegar
¼ cup white wine

salt
2 tsp minced parsley

★ In a sauce pan, combine all ingredients except salt and parsley. Simmer for 10 minutes.

★ Strain. Add salt to taste and minced parsley.

SAUCE PIQUANTE
For game birds, rabbit and antelope.
Volume: 1½ cups

1 Tbsp butter
½ cup chopped onions
¼ cup wine vinegar

1 cup Sauce Espagnole

1 tsp capers
2 tsp minced gherkins
¼ tsp salt ▶

★ In a saucepan, melt the butter and add the onions and wine vinegar. Cook over medium heat until the vinegar is almost gone.

★ Add 1 cup Sauce Espagnole and simmer for 5 minutes.

★ Strain the sauce. Add the capers and gherkins. Season with salt and serve.

Wine Selections

Wine Selections

Over the ages there has been a continuing effort to come up with a perfect schedule of wines to accompany certain foods. Just about everyone who truly loves wine has devised a list for themselves. And just about anyone who knows a little about wines will be willing to give you their schedule — gratis!

But, please, remember that no list devised is the gospel according to Bacchus. It is a guide only, heir to the capriciousness of taste, time and economics. Take the side roads of wine and make your own exciting discoveries, both in cooking and sipping.